Judith Baker Montano

The Crazy Quilt

HANDBOOK

REVISED

2nd Edition

◆ 12 Step-by-Step Projects ◆ Illustrated Stitch Guide

C&T PUBLISHING

Photo by Steven Buckley

Dedication

To my special family who go beyond the call of duty by living with a creative person.

To Fred Montano, who was there for me with the first *Crazy Quilt Handbook* and is still a wonderful father to our children.

To Ernest Shealy, who nurtures and loves us all…best of all, me!

© Copyright 2001 Judith Baker Montano

Developmental Editor: Barbara Konzak Kuhn

Technical Editor: Sara Kate MacFarland

Cover and Book Design: Rose Sheifer

Electronic Illustrations: Jeff Carrillo, Ginny Coull, and Alan McCorkle

Original Art: Judith Baker Montano
© C&T Publishing

Production Assistant: Jeff Carrillo

Copy Editors: Lucy Grijalva and Carol Barrett

Photography for front and back covers: A&I Photography

Photography for chapter openers, page 39: Chris Patterson
page 63: Bill O'Connor

Library of Congress Cataloging-in-Publication Data

Montano, Judith.
 The crazy quilt handbook / Judith Baker Montano.— Revised, 2nd ed.
  p. cm.
Includes bibliographical references and index.
ISBN 1-57120-173-4 (paper trade)
1. Crazy quilts. 2. Patchwork—Patterns. 3. Quilting—Patterns.
4. Fancy work. I. Title.
 TT835 .M658 2001
 746.46—dc21
                                        2001002456

Published by C&T Publishing, Inc.
P.O. Box 1456
Lafayette, California 94549

Printed in Singapore

Table of Contents

Preface

Crazy Quilt Handbook Revision

We are now living in the new millennium, and the original *Crazy Quilt Handbook* has been in print since 1986! I can hardly believe it has been over fifteen years. Many things have changed for me in those years—but crazy quilting has always remained a constant. Publishing technology has also improved and we wanted to update and revise this basic *Crazy Quilt Handbook* with full color and to offer a few new patterns and ideas without losing its basic form, which is a beginning book featuring the Montano Centerpiece Method. We need those basic books which offer help and encouragement plus concise text and illustrations. I hope you enjoy the revision of the *Crazy Quilt Handbook*. For me it was a nostalgic journey and I enjoyed it very much.

Love, Judith

Judith Baker Montano, a Canadian-born fiber artist and the world's leading crazy quilt artist, is an award-winning author of seven books. She incorporates ethnic and traditional influences from world travels into her work, as well as her love of the land and memories of her Alberta ranch home.

Judith started quilting when her family was living in Houston, Texas, where she was an active member of the Kingwood Quilt Guild. Her first prize-winning quilt was made in 1980, when she won Best of Show at the Calgary Exhibition and Stampede in Calgary, Alberta, Canada. It was a special victory, because her great-grandmother had won the same award in 1934.

Crazy quilting has become a constant form of expression for Judith. Her contemporary style is evident in her unique crazy-quilt landscapes, art garments, and accessories, which feature Victorian stitches, beading, silk-ribbon, and punchneedle embroidery. Her garments and quilts have won several design awards in Canada and the U.S. and have been pictured in many national magazines. Judith designs for such companies as Bucilla Corporation, Mokuba Ribbons, Butterick Patterns, and Kanagawa Company. She has appeared on a number of national televison shows, such as HGTV's *Simply Quilts* and *The Carol Duvall Show*. Judith is able to apply her painting and photography skills to her books—making them among the industry's best-selling books.

Judith is a graduate of California State University at Chico, and holds a degree in art and journalism. She enjoys teaching and lecturing, which takes her traveling worldwide at least 150 days of the year. She credits part of her success to the support of the Denver Art Museum and Imelda DeGraw, Curator of Textiles, who helped Judith in creating the original *Crazy Quilt Handbook*. The museum gave Judith her first museum show in 1988, and took her to Japan as an instructor with the 1990 Denver Art Museum Quilt Show in Tokyo. Judith's family includes her husband, Ernest Shealy, and their children Jason, Madeleine, Tara, Dana, Kristen, their spouses, and grandchildren. Judith divides her time between Los Angeles, California and LaVeta, Colorado.

Acknowledgments

This book is the result of many years of study and work. It could never have come about without the support of family and friends. I want to give a special thank you to my husband, Ernest, who is always there with encouragement and help; to my son, Jason, who dares to be a dreamer and is too much like his mother; to my daughter, Madeleine, who is a sweet, creative soul and lover of animals and people; to my special daughters, Kristin—who gives her heart as a teacher and opens a door to learning—and Dana—whose warmth and unconditional love acts as a beacon; and to Tara, who goes at life from a different angle and teaches us all.

A very grateful thank you to my parents, Allen and Joyce, and to my godparents, Uncle Harry and Aunt Muriel. Together, the four of them gave me a wonderful heritage.

I am lucky to have many supportive and interesting friends. I would like to thank Wanda Washington, Frances Lange, Ruth Stonely, Imelda DeGraw, Maren Francis, Alice Bertling, Di Pettigrew, Pat Rogers, Carol Moderi, Chris Nyberg, and Fay Walker. A special thank you to Barb Kuhn, my editor, and Rose Sheifer my designer,—we are always a great team.

Outdoor photography was shot at the Denver Botanic Gardens and at the Montano home.

Photo by Sharon Risedorph

Crazy Quilt Definitions

Crazy quilting can be defined as a method of laying down bits and pieces of fabric in a haphazard fashion and sewing or appliquéing them to a whole cloth. After the whole cloth is completely covered, each seam is covered with decorative details and a combination of embroidery. Unlike a real quilt, a crazy quilt has no batting and is tacked to a whole cloth backing.

Judith Baker Montano, 1986 and 2001

A patchwork quilt without ordered design

Webster's Seventh
New Collegiate Dictionary

…Into them women stitched their long-ings—their hunger for beauty, their impatience with the monotony of their days, their desire for change or adventure, their love for color, which common custom said they might not display in dress. And in the thrill of creating new colors and designing new patterns, daring with cloth and needle to do what someone else had not done, the art of quiltmaking…caused much excitement of fancy in days that would otherwise have been uneventful.

Henderson McDermott
The Farm Journal, circa 1930

Courtesy of Pasadena Historical Museum

Recollections

Crazy quilts have always fascinated me. Though other crafts may distract me, I am always drawn back to the beautiful, outrageous crazy quilts. They remind me of mysterious, glittering jewels, like gypsy cousins peeking out from a patchwork of traditional sister quilts. They are the wild, black-sheep children, tolerated by conservative relatives; perhaps that's why I relate to them. I have always walked to a different drummer.

Crazy quilting is a special love of mine, the answer to my many interests. What other handcraft combines embroidery, sewing, appliqué, laces, ribbons, buttons, beading, painting and color design?

My determination to make crazy quilts began soon after I was married, when we lived in Europe during the 70s. In England, I saw some beautiful Victorian crazy quilts at the Victoria & Albert Museum. They really sparked my interest and I looked about for information on how to make them, but nothing seemed available. So I put it aside and turned toward embellishing clothing. Later, I turned to traditional quilting, but I never lost the longing to make a crazy quilt.

Finally, I decided to teach myself. If the Victorian ladies could make crazy quilts, so could I. Since I couldn't find how-to information, I basically had to teach myself and came up with a machine method of piecing. I've kept my first attempt as a lesson in humility—a very sad vest made from old ties with cotton floss for embroidery (shown below).

Photo by Bill O'Connor

Crazy Quilt c. 1875, United States
Denver Art Museum Collection: Gift of Mrs. J. C. Winn, 1974.151
© Denver Art Museum 2001

Made by Janet Love Harnsberger, c 1885, VA. Courtesy of Janet L. Rose

I worked for five years without guidance. Through trial and error, I learned what works, shortcuts, etc. I learned the Victorian stitches from a basic embroidery book. It was many years, though, before I was invited to teach a class in crazy quilting and then only three people showed up (two of them were my best friends)! Today my classes are filled and the interest is worldwide. The crazy quilt has been accepted...again. Now, in the new millennium, it is accepted as a true art form.

Links with the Past

I believe that one's background and upbringing dictate one's special interests. The texture of my background has a lot to do with my love for crazy quilting.

I was raised on the oldest cattle ranch—the Bar U—in Alberta, Canada, right at the base of the Rocky Mountains. My mother excelled at needlework, pottery, and music. She used these skills to keep us children busy and amused (or tortured, depending on one's view at the time). She taught me needlework at an early age, but I was a terrible child, hiding in the barn so she wouldn't find me, and I was her worst student.

Our ranch was situated next to a Stoney Indian Reservation and a Hutterite colony. (Hutterites are similar to the Amish, but they live in communes and use mechanized farm machinery.) As a girl, I loved to visit our neighbors with my father.

From my Stoney Indian friends, I developed a love for rich, vivid colors and beads. From my Hutterite friends, I gained an admiration for embroidery and needlework. From my father, I developed a great love for the land and the ranching life. Many of those Alberta sunsets find their way into my needlework today.

Crazy quilting is part of my heritage, too, handed down from my Grandmother Baker and

This beautiful antique crazy quilt is from the Kirk Collection, Omaha, Nebraska. Nancy Kirk is president and founder of the Quilt Heritage Foundation and the Crazy Quilt Society. Photo by Steven Buckley.

Photo by Steven Buckley

Great-Grandma Burns. A few years ago, in a chest filled with handiwork, my aunt showed me two lovely crazy quilts made by each woman, tucked away with the tablecloths. They are a wonderful link with the past and my own passion for crazy quilting.

Trailblazers

During the years I worked alone in my studio, crazy quilting everything I could think of, three trailblazers helped bring crazy quilting back to the public's attention. One is Dixie Haywood, who specialized in machine crazy quilting and has

published books on this subject. Another is Dorothy Bond, who has printed a delightful book on Victorian stitches. The third is Penny McMorris, author of a wonderful book on the historical aspects of crazy quilting. Over the last fifteen years, I've done my best to carry the crazy quilt banner. Today there are crazy quilters worldwide, even an international crazy quilt society that meets annually in Omaha, Nebraska.

The Crazy Quilt Handbook touches on the history, stitches, embellishments, and contemporary applications of crazy quilting, as well as my original designs. My goal is to open the door to an old but new and exciting interest, to bring basic crazy quilting to you.

Crazy quilts are fabric documents of history. We can stand in front of an old crazy quilt and see what life was like when the quilt was made. Bits of local and national history combine to give us an overall impression of nineteenth-century life and customs. Lush velvets, satins, and rich silks mix with colorful glazed chintz and cottons. In a crazy quilt, we can see the fabrics of life— those that were used every day and those that were worn only for special occasions. In their method of collage, Victorian crazy quilts are a reflection of the fashions and fads of their time.

Vintage board photo, John Walter Hultquist
From the collection of the author

The Victorian era officially dates from 1837 to 1901, the reign of Britain's beloved Queen Victoria, who gave her name to an age. It was a time when Great Britain was the most powerful nation on earth, with dominions on every continent, and her influence was widespread. Victoria (and her extensive family) dominated the fashion of the times. She was married to Prince Albert, and together they had nine children. Unfortunately, Albert died at a young age, leaving Victoria to spend much of her life in an overdone, maudlin state of widowhood. She collected endless mementos, particularly of her dear departed Albert, until she lived amid a virtual chaos of memorabilia. It finally reached the point at which Victoria held court in the corridors of Windsor Castle because her rooms were too crowded to admit her assembled attendants.

This fussiness was reflected in the fashions of dress and decorating. Women wore tight bodices over huge hoop skirts, topped in the back by large bustles. Ribbons, laces and ruffles appeared in profusion. At home, too, more was better and the best decorators emulated the Queen's clutter.

Crazy quilts were a natural outgrowth of the environment, since needlework was one of a very few "acceptable" occupations for women.

Crazy quilts combined opulent colors, lush fabrics and unrestrained pattern. They also served the sentimental by becoming depositories of all sorts of memorabilia.

Some people question whether the crazy quilt dates from the Victorian era or whether it is indeed the oldest of American quilts. I believe it must be credited to the Victorians. We know the practical, hard-working pioneer woman "discovered" pieced quilts, salvaging every precious bit of cloth to make into bed coverings. Quilted or tied, those were strictly for utility, for the pioneers had no time or materials for frivolous decoration. Crazy quilts require a lot of fabric, especially for base and backing. They were not at all practical, since they were more decorative than warm and were used as "show off" pieces to display in the parlor.

The crazy quilt's heyday was after the Civil War, when the nation came of age and women had more time and money to devote to sewing for pleasure. Decorative art became the rage and every woman strove to create a beautiful home.

The Centennial Exposition of 1876 is a watershed in the development of crazy quilting. Many countries set up elaborate exhibits at the Expo held in Philadelphia. The most popular was the Japanese pavilion—the Victorians were fascinated with the romance and intrigue of Eastern culture. Embroidery books were printed with Oriental designs and these soon appeared in profusion on crazy quilts. The Japanese favored asymmetrical design and this, too, was reflected in the quilts.

Several historians claim the crazy quilt originated with a single Japanese silk screen on display in the Japanese pavilion during the Centennial Exposition. The screen featured a priest walking down a paved walkway. It is thought that needleworkers tried to emulate the paver stones with crazy quilt piecing. Others say the Japanese

Made by Janet Love Harnsberger, c 1885, VA. Courtesy of Janet L. Rose

Victorian crazy quilt from the collection of the Pasadena Historical Museum. Probably made c 1879, Sugar Creek, OH. Courtesy of the Pasadena Historical Museum

"cracked ice" china design that became popular at this time was the inspiration. However it came about, crazy quilting became the first-ever American commercial needlework craze!

For the last quarter of the nineteenth century, crazy quilting was definitely the "in" thing to do. Every woman had to have a crazy quilt. The more intricate and busy it was, the better. It hit every echelon of life, from the poor to the wealthy, to the country and the city woman.

Crazy quilting was a blessing to a number of manufacturers, who encouraged its popularity. Silk makers were delighted with the trend and cashed in by selling pattern books, packets of silk scraps, silk thread and metallics. Women's magazines were full of advice on making crazy quilts, as well as the arts of homemaking.

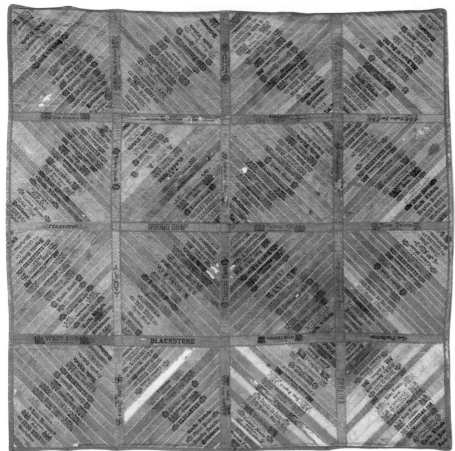

Cover, table c 1880, United States
Denver Art Museum Collection: Gift of Mrs. Andrew Anderson, 1968.41
© Denver Art Museum 2001

This piece is made entirely of yellow cigar silk ribbons, sewn into squares and set together like a Log Cabin "Barn Raising" approximately 37" square. Silks were offered as premiums in boxes of cigars, and many Victorian ladies had large ribbon collections.

This detail shows a Kate Greenaway design used in a Victorian crazy quilt. Miss Greenaway (1846-1901) was a popular English painter & illustrator, best known for drawings of children.

Cigarette silks were prints depicting animals, flags and famous persons of the time that were tucked inside cigarette packets. They were collected and used widely by Victorian quilters.

The Victorian woman did not have such an easy life. She went from belonging to her father to belonging to her husband. She could not vote, there was no birth control, and the average family had eight or nine children. She was not encouraged to attend university. She was schooled in the "womanly arts" (which included running the household, painting, needlework, and cooking). Crazy quilting allowed her to show off her skill in needlework. It was one area in which she could shine.

Even the cigarette manufacturers got into the crazy quilt craze by producing small rectangular silk ribbons, which were "giveaways" in cigarette and cigar packages.

The ribbons featured celebrities of the era—actors, opera stars and politicians—as well as animals, national flags, Native Americans, royalty and city flags. Although the Victorian woman was not allowed to smoke, she certainly encouraged the male members of the household to do so—and many silks were woven into crazy quilts to tell us about Victorian life.

Some of the quilts are highlighted with intricate oil paintings on velvet, which often depict flowers, animals and Kate Greenaway children. Many original paintings represent family members and pets, but most of these designs were taken from pattern books.

The most common embellishment technique was embroidery. Animals, birds, children and flowers were favorite Victorian motifs, as were Japanese designs. Many designs were taken from patterns that were perforated so the motif could be outlined on the fabric with a white powder. With a sharp needle, a picture magazine and a stamping pounce filled with powder, a crazy quilter could sew any kind of embroidery design.

Remember that a special function of these quilts was to serve as a personal scrapbook. Important dates are often embroidered, as are the initials of the maker or of loved ones. Birthdays, weddings and deaths are commemorated in lovely italicized embroideries. Mementos of special occasions decorate the quilts, with bits of clothing fabrics and handkerchiefs incorporated into the quilts.

Most Victorian crazy quilts were made as a throw. They were used for display in the parlor, thrown over the back of the sofa or draped over the piano. Sometimes they were displayed on the wall. They were there to be admired and to add to the decor.

The Victorian woman was busy from morning to night with large households and families, which took a great deal of care. During the Age of Industrialization, cloth was readily available and things were made a bit easier, but it also brought about a dilemma for the Victorian woman. One of the things related to wealth is leisure time and related to leisure time is needlework. So behind every young ambitious man working his way up the ladder to success was a woman working to produce a crazy quilt to show off in the parlor to prove just how successful they were!

Crazy quilting was also used for smaller items. Pillows and table runners were popular and added greatly to the parlor decor. Many were framed with velvet borders and silk ruffles, or highlighted with borders of elaborate crochet. A piano was a fixture in a well-furnished Victorian

Souvenir ribbons of campaigns and special events were often sewn into crazy quilts.

home and a piano scarf was often an ideal showcase for crazy quilting.

Farm and country women did not have easy access to silks and other fancy fabrics, but this certainly did not diminish their love for crazy quilting. These humble crazy quilts were made mostly of wool, cottons, and a few special fabrics. Some farm women worked like men in the

Printed silks, like this one from an antique Victorian quilt, were quick and easy ways to achieve a pictorial effect. Any fabric print, appliquéd onto a fabric base and edged with embroidery stitches, can be used this way.

long evenings to complete. Her name was Bessie Burns Baker and she loved needlework. Her own mother was a master quilter. Though she worked hard all day, my father and his sister remember her working by lamplight over her quilt. My grandparents emigrated from Oklahoma and Kansas to take up farming near Cayley, Alberta, Canada. We can only imagine the long, hard hours and the loneliness.

Some of the fabrics in my grandmother's quilt are disintegrating, but it still has a story to tell. Past memories and future hopes are woven into this quilt. It includes pieces of her dresses, suiting from my grandfather's best suit and shirting from those he wore in the fields. One

piece is from a baby dress that belonged to little Agnes, their first daughter who died at age five. A special handkerchief, brought back from the Great War by an uncle, is proudly displayed.

This crazy quilt is not as lush or fancy as other crazy quilts, but it is just as much a document of history, a tribute to a young farm wife who labored to create something beautiful for her home.

fields, but still found time for needlework. Their crazy quilts are a tribute to every woman's basic need to beautify her surroundings.

My grandmother was such a country woman, and her crazy quilt was made in 1932. It took her many

Quilt (and detail) photo by Bill O'Connor

This is the 1930s crazy quilt made by the author's grandmother, Bessie Burns Baker. Above right is a closeup look at a World War 1 souvenir handkerchief from the quilt. Above left is a photo of Mrs. Baker with the author's father as a baby. Courtesy of Mr. and Mrs. S. Lange

Revival

Just as in Victorian times, we can use crazy quilting in our lives today. Our philosophies of fashion and interior design are now very flexible and we can live with whatever pleases us.

Friendship quilt made by the author from fabric pieces given to her by friends from the Kingwood Quilt Guild.

Interior Design and Accessories

The country and traditional look that swept the 1980s introduced a slightly cluttered look in many homes, reminiscent of Victorian days. It is quite fashionable now to mix old with new, pattern on pattern and a whole palette of colors. Crazy quilting fits right in.

By using all solid colors and relatively larger shapes a crazy quilt can be very sophisticated. In this case, instead of a traditional square, the quilt can be a rectangular banner, hung above eye level.

Pillows are a fast and easy way to make a decorative statement. Crazy quilting makes effective pillows in heart, fan, and round shapes (use washable cottons—be sure they're prewashed). A good blend of fabrics and colors makes a versatile table setting.

Let your imagination guide you in decorating with crazy quilting. It can be a dramatic focus of a room or a special, colorful accent.

Family Heirlooms and Mementos

Crazy quilting is a great way to commemorate important occasions. By using special fabrics and lace, and adding special dates and initials, a framed piece can become a family treasure.

A wall hanging fits any decor and can be the collection point for family mementos. Use handkerchiefs, laces, hair ribbons, fabrics from special garments and fabric painting to create a unique family tribute.

Friendship Quilts

The crazy quilt is a perfect vehicle for a group effort such as a friendship quilt. Forty friends in my Texas quilt guild contributed fabric pieces to a surprise going-away gift for me that kept me busy and happy assembling my crazy quilt in my new home. We all shared the pleasure when it won Judges' Choice at the Colorado State Fair. The ease of incorporating little pieces of special things, dates and initials and assembling assorted shapes and sizes of fabric make a crazy quilt an ideal project for guilds and church groups.

Jewelry and Clothing

Not all of us have time to make quilts, but we can work crazy quilting into smaller projects such as clothing, accessories, and jewelry. This needlework technique makes wonderful pendants and collars. Pendants can be made in any shape or size if you use my special method of putting pendants together. Crazy quilt jewelry is not only wonderful to wear, but it makes a very personal gift, too. Just remember to keep the fabric pieces proportionately small—a 4" pendant is much more effective with several small, irregular shapes than with just two or three larger pieces of fabric.

There are several popular books devoted to personalized clothing and patterns that adapt well to special techniques. The versatility of crazy quilting allows you to personalize a garment for your mood or lifestyle. Colors can be vibrant or subdued, fabrics can be glitzy or soft, sophisticated and elegant or country and homespun.

Create Your Own Look

Country

To achieve the casual, natural look of country life, use homespun, checks, plaids, wool suiting, cottons, calicos, and lightweight denims. Keep the fabrics in medium intensities (dusty) to give an antique, faded aura. Tea-dye the laces and use old pearl buttons.

Southwest

The desert look of soft earth tones, spectacular sunsets, and turquoise and silver reflects a way of life as well as a region. Work the crazy quilt pieces with desert colors like terra cotta, dusty pink, and sage green. Use leather and textured fabrics like Ultrasuede® and nubby silk. Embellish the pieces with tribal fetishes, silver ornaments, and buttons.

City Sophistication

Use solid colors to give a contemporary look. Work in large geometric shapes and embroider with silk threads or ribbon in one color. Emphasize the stitch design by using a single stitch throughout the piece. Work in monochromatic or one-color schemes—white on white or black on black. Use the play of texture and shine to create interest. Highlight eveningwear with embroidery and beading.

Victoriana

Re-create the antique Victorian look by using rich colors in satin, silk and velvet (cotton velveteen handles best). Achieve the cluttered look by overlapping layers of lace and ribbons, embroidery, beading, and ornaments. Antique laces and doilies can meander across the piece. Allow the embroidery, lace, and ribbon lines to "run over" each other. Use actual antique buttons and trinkets, or re-create the look with modern brass doodads and mother-of-pearl buttons.

With our easy access to all kinds of fabrics and threads, it seems right that crazy quilting should take its place in the evolution of contemporary quilting. It lets us show off our needlework, document our way of life and, above all, preserve our family histories and traditions. Crazy quilting is truly the most painterly of all the quilting techniques.

Getting Started

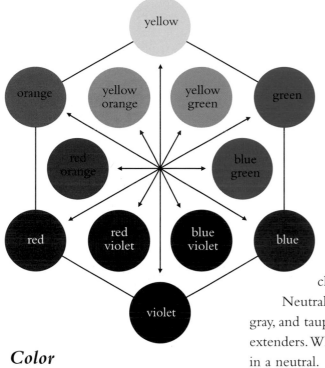

Use of color is a very personal choice and the most difficult one for many. The best inspiration for successful color combination is the world of nature. The colors in flowers and animals, sunrises and sunsets are beautiful examples of effective, varied combinations. The Color Wheel is often used to illustrate color combinations found in nature.

Color

The color wheel can help you understand the logistics of mixing color. Everything begins with three primary colors—red, yellow and blue. By mixing equal amounts, we create secondary colors—orange, green and violet (purple). Tertiary colors are made by mixing a primary and secondary color next to it.

The excitement of color is making combinations that work. The wheel illustrates the four combinations most often found in nature.

- A monochromatic color scheme uses a single color, perhaps varied with tints and shades of that color.
- An analogous color scheme combines neighboring colors on the wheel, such as blue and blue-green or red and red-orange.
- Complementary colors are opposite each other on the wheel, such as red and green or purple and yellow.

- A triad uses three colors spaced equidistant on the wheel, such as orange, purple and green.

Adding a neutral to any combination extends it without changing its basic effect. Neutrals are black, white, gray, and taupe. Think of these as extenders. When in doubt, throw in a neutral.

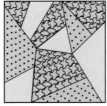 

This fabric is dark when surrounded by light fabrics.   *The same fabric is light when surrounded by darker ones.*

Intensity

Intensity is the brightness or dullness of a color. Any color is brightest in its natural state (closest to primary). To change the intensity, or make it duller, the color is mixed with its complement. For example, if we have red and want to dull it, we mix it with green. To change the intensity of the blue, mix it with orange. By adding more orange, you eventually get rust. A color is dullest when mixed with an equal amount of the complementary color.

Value

The value of any color is changed by adding white or black.

Adding white lightens the color to a tint, while black darkens it to a shade. For example, pink and burgundy are light and dark values of red.

When both white and black are added to the primary color, the result is a grayed color.

A color's value is affected by the colors around it. In crazy quilting, the same fabric may read dark in one place and light in another, depending on the nature of its neighbors. A light fabric, surrounded by darker ones, seems to come forward; a dark fabric, surrounded by lighter ones, appears to recede.

Crazy quilting doesn't give you license to throw in every color, without rhyme or reason. Using the color wheel is a sure way to select an effective combination of colors. I like to use two complementary colors, with one or two neutrals. I decide on the intensity and value of these colors, combining a good mix of prints, solids and textured fabrics. I usually work with two complementary colors, or a triad, and I break my values into Pastels, Dusties, and Jewel Tones.

Sort out the jumble of your fabrics and arrange them in color groups. Storing fabric in color groups makes color selection easier and more efficient. This way, you can reach for your stack or bundle of blues and find all the solids, textures and patterns in one place. Keep neutrals grouped together, too.

Repetition and Balance

Repetition and balance go hand in hand; we cannot have one without the other. Achieve a balance by repeating color, pattern and/or texture. To emphasize a particular shape or color, for example, you will achieve balance of design by repeating the shape (or color) throughout the work. Asymmetrical design uses uneven numbers for balance—better asymmetrical than overall design. It is more pleasing to the eye.

If a vest has a design on the back, try to have it fall over one shoulder. This offers a bit of a surprise, while following principles of repetition and balance. Repeating the design at the bottom of the other side adds to the overall effect.

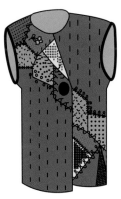

Perhaps the vest has crazy quilt fans on the front. To balance the design, have the fans spill over from one side to the other in uneven numbers. By repeating the fans

over the surface of the vest, you will achieve an asymmetrical, yet balanced design. Color can be a unifying factor.

If you want a "scenic" crazy quilt vest, draw the scene across the front and balance the design by carrying the color across both sides. Further balance is achieved by repeating stitches from side to side.

Texture, Pattern, and Solids

In crazy quilting, it is very important to have a balance of texture and pattern. If you have too many busy prints, the fancy stitches won't show up. It is important to bounce printed pieces off solids or textured, solid fabrics. This adds interest and shows the pattern to best advantage. The same is true of textured fabrics. If your crazy quilt is made up only of textured fabrics, the texture is taken for granted, and the fancy stitches get lost in the nap of some textures. In order for each fabric piece to harmonize with its neighbors, they must complement each other in color, texture, and finish.

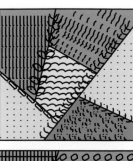

All texture, which is very boring; stitches tend to blend in and get lost.

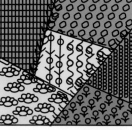

All pattern, which loses the stitches

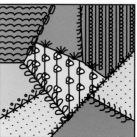

A balance of texture, solids and pattern

- Fabrics in the texture category include satin, moiré, wool, nubby fabrics, tweed, velvets or any fabric that has a special feel to it.
- Prints include any fabric that has a pattern, such as a pin dot, calico, decorator floral, cross hatching, even stripes.
- Solids can be textured or smooth. They can be shiny or matte. Jacquard weaves of shiny and matte are read as solids.

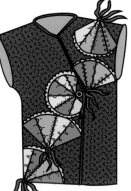

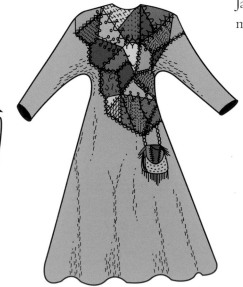

Important Rule:

In traditional crazy quilting I have one cardinal rule: Never put pattern against pattern, and always "bounce" patterns against solids and textured solids.

Selecting Fabrics

Crazy quilting uses an infinite variety of fabrics. Virtually anything, from velvets to cottons, from lace to drapery fabric, can find its way into crazy quilting.

At the fabric store you can find polyesters, cottons, satins, silks, and wool. Dress-weight velvets are great for many projects, especially cotton velveteen.

Be aware that high-nap fabrics can be difficult to work with, and may be very heavy. Your best buys will be on the bargain tables; a half yard piece won't interest a dressmaker, but you can use it for many crazy quilt projects. Lace fabrics and sheers, used as overlays, might fit your project. Even plaids can be worked into crazy quilting.

A good source for cottons is the specialty quilt shop. Drapery shops are a good source of glazed chintz as well as moiré and decorator cottons. Drapery-weight moiré is soft and manageable and has a better feel than most dress weights. If you buy drapery fabric, be sure it is pliable and lightweight, and will press into shape without creating a lumpy ridge in your work.

Before setting your heart on a particular fabric, consider its practicality. For some garments, you'll want washable fabric. Be sure these are preshrunk before you work with them. Fancier fabrics, such as satin, must be dry cleaned.

Because crazy quilting uses relatively small pieces, you can usually buy quarter to half yard lengths. If a piece is a large decorator print with lots of color and design, you might buy a yard or more. Neutral colors that you'll use again and again might be purchased in longer lengths, too.

Old ties are terrific for crazy quilting. They can be quite inexpensive and, since most are a Jacquard weave, the reverse design is on the back and you get two designs for the price of one.

All crazy quilting starts with a base or foundation, usually of preshrunk muslin. The foundation is always covered, front and back, so you can use up old fabric pieces for the foundation. A base of cotton is particularly desirable for garments, because it drapes better than heavier fabrics.

Crazy Quilt, 1878-1880, Julia Addie Adams
Denver Art Museum Collection: Gift of Rae S. Simmons, 1982.133
© Denver Art Museum 2001

The great charm of crazy quilting is that there is no pattern, and you can think like a painter. If you've decided on a color palette and selected your materials carefully, you've already laid the cornerstone of the finished piece. I think of the piecing as the first colorwash in a watercolor painting. As you sew, make sure the pieces complement each other in color and fabric type. The outcome is your own individual interpretation.

Plastic "Window" Templates

You may have seen an artist squint through a small circle he's made with his hands. By doing this, he eliminates all the surrounding distractions to concentrate on his subject.

Quilters can do something similar with window templates. Using template plastic (generally available at quilt shops), cut out a window the exact size and shape of the finished project. This window lets you see only the design area, eliminating the distraction of unfinished edges, seam allowances, etc. The crazy quilt foundation is always cut larger than the pattern outline. While this allows for shrinkage, it also give you room to play with design placement. By moving the window around on the foundation, twisting and angling it, you can choose just the right combination of color and shape.

Antique Method

In some Victorian crazy quilts, the edges of the individual piece were left unturned and tacked down only with the embroidery stitches. This was not very satisfactory as the edges raveled and did not stand up to use. In most cases, edges were turned under and appliquéd down.

Curved lines were thought to be more desirable than long, angular lines. Some Victorian pattern books suggested that larger pieces could be basted in place on the foundation and the smaller pieces fitted in. (Remember the paver stones?)

The Victorians always sewed the fabric pieces to a foundation. Most often, the work was done in small squares which were sewn together to make a large piece. The squares made for easier piecing and embroidery. Once sewn together, the seam lines would also be embroidered.

Hiding Seam Lines

Many stitchers did not like to see a line where the squares joined and

The Doukakis Family Quilt, made by Jan Doukakis, 1997. A modern crazy quilt made by the Antique Method. Courtesy Jan Doukakis

would appliqué patches to cover seams. I use a similar method when I'm joining the pieces of a garment (the fronts and back of a vest, for example). At the side and shoulder seams, I leave the fabric at the outer edge hanging out over the seam line on one side. When it's time to sew up the seam, I peel back the loose edges, exposing the muslin backing. After the seams are sewn and the jagged edges are pressed flat over the seam, the loose edges are appliquéd onto the adjacent piece, completely hiding the seam line. (See Overlapping, page 26)

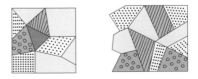

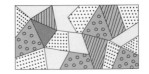

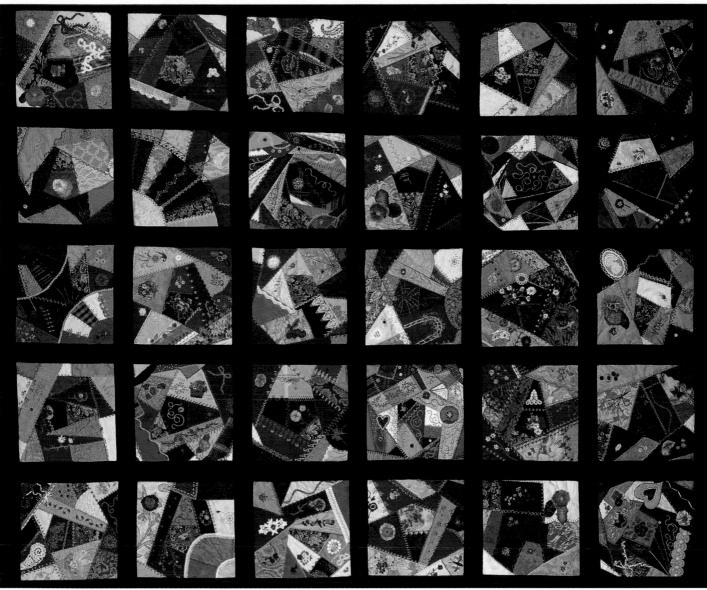

San Fernando Valley Quilt Association group quilt made with Montano Centerpiece Method. Courtesy Pasadena Historical Museum

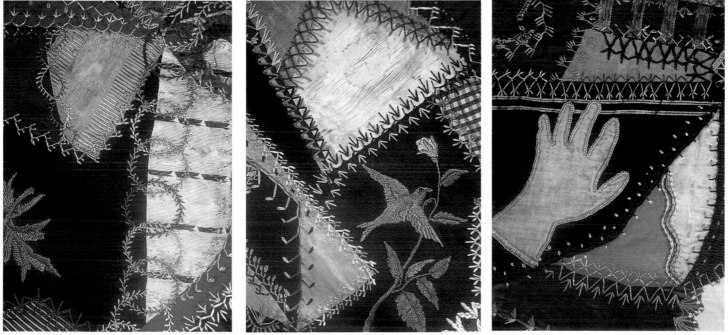

These details are from a quilt made by Frances Ann Hoffhines, c 1884. Courtesy of her grand-daughter, Jean Kent

Photos by Judith Baker Montano

21

The Montano Methods

My machine piecing is done in a string quilting fashion, sewing each piece onto its neighbors. The difference is I strive for a crazy quilt effect, not string quilting. Curved edges are turned under to be appliquéd later. It is not necessary to press each fabric before it is sewn down, because it will be heavily pressed afterwards. Press each seam line before the next piece is added.

I have two methods for sewing down fabrics to a foundation (which is cut ½" larger than the desired finished size). On smaller items, start with a center piece and work around it. On larger pieces, larger than 12" squares, it is usually best to start in a corner and work outward in a fan-like progression. We will go through each method step-by-step. Remember, we are using a fold-over-and-press method, but we are striving for a mosaic look to our piecing. We want to avoid a "strippy" look.

Montano Centerpiece Method

Use this method for small items such as purses and jewelry.

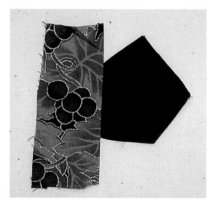

1. Cut a small piece with five angled sides from dark, solid fabric. (A dark fabric is preferable because it recedes and brings the eye to the center, making a good base for embroidery.) Pin the piece onto the foundation at the center for small pendants, offset it for larger pieces.

3. Sew from one edge of Angle 1 to the end. Flip the rectangle over to its right side, trim out from the seam, and press.

2. Cut a wide rectangle. Lay it along Angle 1, right sides together.

4. Cut a second wide rectangle and lay it against Angle 2. If you are right-handed, work clockwise, as shown. If you are left-handed, work counterclockwise. Be sure to cover the previous piece. Sew from the edge of the previous piece to the edge of the second angle. Cut out from behind and press flat.

5. Continue around until all the angles of the center piece are covered. Note that on Angle 5, the wide rectangle must extend over the pieces that cover both Angle 1 and Angle 4. This is a good place to use a pieced rectangle.

7. Continue adding rectangular pieces in a clockwise or counterclockwise direction. Keep a good balance of color, texture, pattern, and solids as you work. Remember to press as you go. Always use rectangular pieces and cut back to shapes and sizes after each cycle.

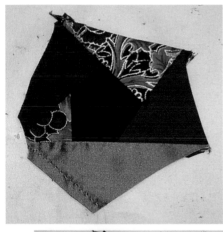

6. Now cut more angles from the pieces you have sewn down. Be sure to work toward a variety of shapes and sizes.

Photos by Judith Baker Montano

1. Cut a corner fabric patch with three angled sides. Pin it in place flush with the bottom right corner of the foundation fabric.

2. Select the next piece of fabric. Cut it into a wide (about 3") rectangle. Lay it edge to edge on Angle 1, right sides together. Sew through the two pieces and the foundation fabric, from one end of Angle 1 to the other. Trim the seam. Flip the rectangle piece over to its right side and press. If a tail of fabric hangs out, don't be concerned; it will be trimmed off after the next piece is sewn down.

3. Cut wide rectangles as you go. Be sure to alternate the colors as well as solids and patterns. Select the next fabric and lay it on Angle 2, making sure it extends over the previously sewn piece.

4. Sew from the outside edge of the previous piece to the edge of Angle 2. Trim away the excess fabric, then flip the piece to the right side and press.

5. Choose another rectangle. Cover Angle 3 and the piece just sewn down in the same manner. Trim out from behind, flip over, and press. Now you've completed the first clockwise level of the fan.

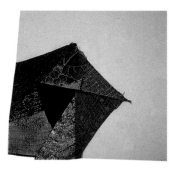

The next step is very important. You must stop to cut angles from the rectangles just sewn down. Make sure you cut a variety of shapes and sizes. Then, starting at the top of the last piece sewn, begin working counter-clockwise to lay down the next level. If you come to a long run, or your work is becoming too strippy, refer to the Problem Solving section (page 26) for piecing rectangles.

6. Continue to fan back and forth, right to left, then left to right, until the foundation is completely filled. Always trim the excess fabric from the seams to keep the work from bulking up. Cut angles after each "cycle," making sure you have a variety of shapes and sizes.

There are five basic elements in the recipe for successful crazy quilting. By using the right mix of color, repetition, balance, fabrics (solids and patterns) and embellishment, you will be happy with the result. The ideas discussed here relate to virtually any project, regardless of size or intended use. I will often refer to a vest as an example, but the same principles apply to full-size quilts, framed pictures, etc., as well as to garments.

Because so many people like to embellish clothing with crazy quilting, let's begin with a brief look at garment patterns.

Photo by Alan Carter

Adapting Crazy Quilting to Garment Patterns

Choose patterns that have flat areas for embellishment or high interest areas, such as borders or a yoke, that will showcase crazy quilting. The lines of the garment should be simple so as not to compete with the crazy quilting. Darts pose an obvious problem but they are not impossible and I use them in most of my designs.

When you find a suitable pattern, it is best to buy it right away because pattern companies are constantly changing their lines. Purchase the usual pattern size; crazy quilting does not affect the fit of the garment.

Begin with a Bigger Base

Work with a foundation that is larger than the actual pattern. For example, if I am going to crazy quilt the yoke of a vest or blouse, I transfer the yoke outline onto a base of muslin or cotton outing. On this foundation, I draw the actual seam lines, but I cut out the shape ½" larger all around. This allows for shrinkage that may occur with piecing. This is a principle I use in all crazy quilting, whether the piece is to be a dress, a pillow or a pendant.

Design Placement

Often you will see a garment that has obviously taken many hours to produce, but it isn't very flattering.

Maybe the stitcher has produced a Folded Star vest. The colors are lovely and she's very proud of it. But where is the star? Smack dab in the middle of her back, and it's a perfect target! Perhaps the same stitcher makes a Folded Star jacket. It is very nice and the quilting is superb, but it reminds us of a German opera star with an iron bra because the two stars are placed on either side of the jacket front, drawing attention to her bosom!

Our proud stitcher (who has enough padding of her own) makes

Illustration by Ann Davis Nunemacher

a warm winter jacket, using ultra-loft batting that makes her look twice as big. To top it off, she uses a bright, geometric quilt pattern, so the effect makes her look like a moving quilt. Perhaps her jacket is a virtuoso work of Seminole patchwork, but the horizontal bands around the bottom bring attention to her ample hips.

Ever seen a quilter walking around with her arms up in the air? It's because all her handiwork wound up under the arms!

If it seems that I'm familiar with this unfortunate lady, it's because I've described myself. I have made all these mistakes and learned the hard way an important lesson: *position the crazy quilting where it will be seen, but not in a place where the attention doesn't suit the wearer of the garment.*

Try to have a center of interest in every garment. It can be up on one shoulder, or down at the hem on one side. Everything then works out from this center of interest. Perhaps you want to focus on a special fabric or embroidery. If this is the case, be sure the rest of the crazy quilting complements it, without overshadowing it.

Problem Solving

As you work back and forth sewing fabrics to a foundation, you will sometimes find yourself in a situation you can't get out of. Here are some tips and suggestions for working your way out of a difficult spot.

Fans

Fans fill a "V." Many beginners will find they have worked into a "V" angle that is difficult to fill in. If this happens, take advantage of it by sewing in a fan. Following the existing angle, just add long, narrow triangles until you work out of the "V." The last side of the last triangle will have to be appliquéd down.

Fans were a favorite Victorian motif and are very easy to make. They can be of irregular shape or very even, pointed or curved. A fan shape gives a sense of movement and can cover a large area. They are great corner fillers, too. A fan can be pre-sewn and added to the foundation as a whole unit, or you can sew it in piece by piece as shown below.

Pre-Piecing

Pre-pieced rectangles fill in long lines. After you've added a few pieces, some of the lines may tend to get very long. I create a piece of fabric to fill the space by sewing several shapes together, then sew them to the foundation as a unit. I sew triangles and squares together in a long rectangle.

To create angles in a strip, cut one rectangle end at the desired angle (use the heavier fabric of the two pieces). Lay it along the second rectangle, as you want it to look in your finished piece. Now fold the piece under the angled piece, down along the cut angle. Press with your fingers, turn over, and slip your thumb under the back flap. Now sew along the angle using the pressed line as a guide.

Overlapping

Curves shorten lines. Long lines can be shortened with curved edges. Just about any curve must be hand appliquéd onto its neighbor, after straight machine sewing is done.

Press under the seam allowance on the curved edge. Sew the straight edge of the piece onto the foundation, but leave the curved edge loose. Trace the curve onto the foundation, then flip the curved fabric back, out of the way of your sewing. Continue on with the crazy quilting, extending pieces just inside the traced curve. When the curved piece is smoothed down and appliquéd in place, it will cover the raw edges. This works for both concave and convex shapes.

Photos by Steven Buckley

Embellishments

For most people, this is the best part of crazy quilting, and the most satisfying.

This is the process that turns an interesting base piece into something exotic and magical. When it comes to embellishment details, my motto is, "The more, the better," and sometimes it is only when I run out of time or money that I decide to stop!

I use less lace and ribbon on clothing and accessories, by personal choice, and never ruffles, because they add too much bulk to my figure. On these designs I try to emphasize embroidery instead. Laces, bows and ruffles are fine for items such as wall hangings and pillows since they are not handled as much and can carry more frills.

Embellishments can be divided into those that are done before the base work and those done after. Embellishments done before sewing are the larger, more ambitious decorations such as embroidery pictures, calligraphy, painting, photo transfer and punchneedle embroidery. These are usually worked onto larger pieces of fabric that can be trimmed and shaped to fit into the piecework.

Once the foundation is complete, work in a set order of sequence—this saves much time and trouble. Think like a painter (after all, you are creating a one-of-a-kind art project!). When you are laying down the layers of embellishments, it is no different from when the painter lays down layers of color wash. First, add the lace, ribbons and trims. Then, cover the remaining seams with embroidery. When all the embroidery is done, the beading is next. Add buttons last, as they are usually bulkiest.

We will look at each technique in turn, beginning with those enhancements generally done before the basework. Don't feel that you have to incorporate a little bit of everything; choose the decorative details that you like the best and that are most appropriate to your project.

Embroideries

Embroidery is the main focal point in crazy quilting. The last chapter of this book features Victorian stitches and variations that can be used to cover seams and embellish narrow fabric strips. Other types of embroidery, however, can be used to create a rich variety of design effects. These are among the few decorative elements you can pre-plan and complete before sewing the foundation.

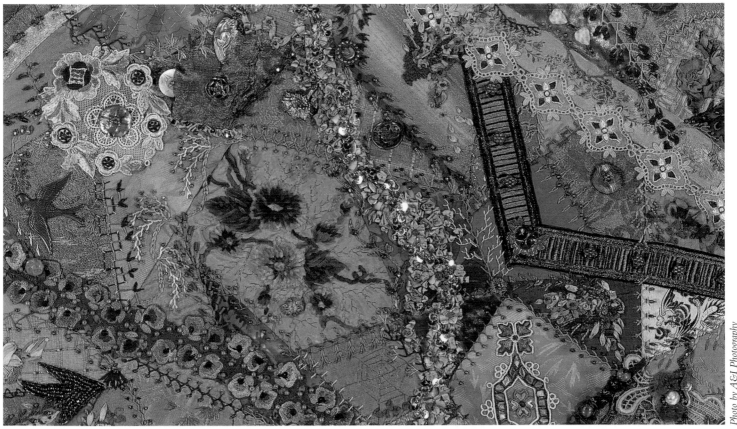

"Victorian Romance" by Judith Baker Montano

Photo by A&I Photography

Cross-Stitch

A cross-stitch piece is a good, easy way to incorporate your name, a date, or a favorite stitched design into crazy quilting. You can create your own cross-stitch motif or select one from a favorite cross-stitch design book. A cross-stitch piece can be an excellent center focus for a project made to honor a graduation, wedding or new baby, complete with name, dates and other statistics. Cross-stitch fabrics come in a wide variety of weaves and colors.

Detail from Kingwood quilt

Outline Embroidery

Victorian crazy quilts feature a multitude of outline embroideries. Animals, children and flowers were favorite motifs. Many of the Victorian embroidery patterns are still available today, along with more modern design books. The Stem stitch is used for outline embroidery and is much like drawing a line. When used properly, it makes a fine line (see Stitch Dictionary, page 72.)

Use tissue paper and a transfer pencil to transfer the design onto your fabric, and your design books will remain intact. If your fabric is light enough, you can see the design through the fabric to trace (a sunny window is a great help in this, for those who do not own a lightbox). Some favorite motifs are outline drawings of hands or baby feet. Duplicate a child's drawing for a juvenile project, or borrow ideas from a coloring book, a special pet or place.

Outline embroidery is the technique most frequently used to create pictorial scenes in crazy quilting.

Satin Stitch

The Victorian stitcher was an expert at this stitch, and it often appears in crazy quilts. They used silk threads and usually padded the satin stitch to give it dimension. Use this stitch to make a special feature in your piece. (See Stitch Dictionary page 66)

Crewel Embroidery

Crewel work is generally worked with fine wool. It derives its name from a firm, two-ply needlework wool also known as crewel. This type of embroidery tends to favor flowers and animals. It is traditionally worked with a tapestry needle. I like to use the crewel stitches with silk threads, especially the long and short Straight stitch. It fills in very fast. Refer to *Elegant Stitches* for more embroidery stitches.

Antique quilt

Silk Ribbon Embroidery

This wonderful embroidery is worked with a chenille or tapestry needle, using a 4mm silk ribbon. Very dimensional, it adds texture and interest to your crazy quilt. It is always worked in a hoop, but I have often added it after piecing. (See Bibliography, page 80.)

Silk ribbon embroidery for box lid, by author

Punchneedle Embroidery

Punchneedle embroidery is an old Russian technique that uses a hollow needle. They come in several sizes, and a variety of threads can be used. The fabric is stretched, drum tight, in an embroidery hoop but the design is worked from the back. The result is a carpet of tiny loops that create the design on the right side. The loops can be sheared to give a velvety look. The work is very durable and washable. Metallic threads can be used to good effect with this technique.

Antique Painting on fabric

Punchneedle embroidery can be used to highlight a pattern in a fabric. If the design of the fabric shows through to the back, you can follow the lines to punchneedle parts of the pattern. The beauty of this technique is that it's very fast and pretty. Any embroidery pattern can be used, even line drawings from coloring books and magazines.

Calligraphy

Those blessed with fine penmanship, or who have taken a course in calligraphy, can add poetry, quotations and/or signatures to their crazy quilting. Use a fine-line pen that is permanent and washable. It's not a bad idea to test the pen on scrap fabric first. Even the most non-artistic can use this type of pen to trace line drawings that can be included in the piecework.

Fabric Painting

Victorian women were often trained in the fine art of watercolors and oil painting. A popular pastime was oil painting on velvet and silk. Today, we have acrylic paints that are more suitable to fabric painting. They can be used right out of the tube for a painterly look, or watered down and used like watercolor. These paints dry very quickly and can be painted over in a matter of minutes. Be sure the paint doesn't dry on the brush, because it won't come out and the brush will be ruined. For wall hangings and pictures that won't be handled, set the painting by pressing it, from the back, into a towel. If the piece will be actively used, then set it by soaking a cloth in vinegar and using it as a pressing cloth over the painting.

Antique Painting on fabric

Fabric Painting by Alice Bertling, done as a gift for the author.

29

Fabric dyed by author. Marbleized fabric purchased at art show by author.

Marbleizing

Marbleized fabrics are swirled with colors, and by doing it yourself, you can work in the colors of your choice. The process uses acrylic paint and carrageenan (a suspension medium), mixed so that the paint floats on the surface of the water.

Materials
- Distilled water
- Silk fabric, or cotton solid
- Acrylic paints
- Aluminum ammonium sulfate
- Plastic cups for paint
- Toothpicks
- Narrow strips of newspaper
- Large aluminum roasting pan
- A comb as wide as the marbleizing pan
- Carrageenan

Pre-treat the fabric in a mixture of 1 pint hot water, with 2 Tbsp. of aluminum ammonium sulfate.

Procedure
- In a blender, add one tsp. of carrageenan to one quart moving water. Blend for 1 minute.
- Pour into the marbleizing pan.
- Mix the paint in a cup with distilled water, until it is the consistency of thin cream. Use a separate cup for each color.
- Dip a toothpick into paint. Lightly touch the paint to water surface. Work with several colors.
- Use the comb to swirl the paint (knock out a few teeth on the comb for wider designs).
- Lay the fabric right side up on the painted surface. Lift up gently.
- Lay on paper towels to dry.
- Pick up remaining paint in the pan with strips of newspaper, and start again.

Fabric Dyes

Some fabric dyes are suitable for painting and they lend a wonderful quality to the work. Check at your local craft shop for these products. The dye is applied with a paint brush, just like regular paints, and is permanent.

Fabric dyeing gives you more control over the colors of your project, particularly if you want a wide range of shadings. The dye is diluted with water, yet the colors can still be bright and wonderful. Dye, however, marks everything it touches, so it is best to work in a controlled environment. This is not a project for the kitchen counter with small children and pets underfoot! Work with a sheet of plastic over your worktable and use rubber gloves.

If you want to try fabric dyeing, see if your local craft store or guild offers a class. There are variations to this process, in which the dye is applied to wet fabric. The intensity of the color usually pales as the fabric dries.

Photo by Steven Buckley

Photography on Fabric

Photographs, old and new, can be transferred to fabric with several procedures. We have come a long way technologically, and I suggest you buy a book on photo-to-fabric transfer instructions. Please be aware of copyright laws when you are working with images other than your family's photos! Use family pictures or antique photos with good contrast, and the results will be great.

Ink-Jet Printer Method

Those of you with more computer knowledge than I can print directly onto fabric using an ink jet printer. Simply scan the image into the computer, iron the chosen fabric onto freezer paper, and feed it through the printer.

Ribbons and Roses

The variety of ribbon offered today makes crazy quilting more fun than ever.

The widest ribbon can be sewn like a fabric piece right onto the base work, while some ribbons can meander across the seams, or be folded into floral shapes.

Very narrow ribbon can be woven through lace or twisted and tacked down with French knots.

Metallic and printed ribbons add to the effects of color, pattern and texture. Don't overlook velvet ribbon, which will add wonderful texture, and the wonderful organza ribbon which will add a sheer and airy texture to your work.

Embellishment on Ribbons

I often use a satin ribbon as an appliqué piece. Making sure to hide the ends under the folded or seamed edges. These act as a background for buttons, beads, and embroidery stitches, such as the Feather stitch, and various Victorian stitches. Use embroidery floss that contrasts nicely with the ribbon.

Australian Photo Method

Materials

- Photocopy or picture (must be a photocopy made with dry toner, not a laser or color copy print)
- Pure gum turpentine
- Blotting paper
- Large metal spoon
- Cotton balls
- Natural fabric, such as cotton batiste or silk—no polyester

Process

Place the blotting paper on a table. Lay the silk (after it has been well pressed and is wrinkle free) down on the blotting paper. Lay the photocopy face down on the silk.

Dip a cotton ball into the turpentine (don't get it soppy wet) and rub the back of the photocopy until it becomes opaque.

Take the spoon in one hand and hold the photocopy firmly in place with the other hand. Rub the back of the photocopy very hard with the spoon.

Carefully lift up a corner of the paper to check the image. If the image is faint, rub on a bit more turpentine and burnish with the spoon again.

Remove the photocopy. Iron the image into the silk. You may color the image with watercolors or acrylic paints.

Photo Transfer Method

You can buy photo transfer paper from computer stores to make your own transfers. Simply scan the chosen image into your computer, and print the image onto the photo transfer paper. This will be a reversed image. Many copy centers will do this for you, and will be able to mirror the image, so it is printed with the correct orientation.

Photos by Steven Buckley

The author's granddaughter, Kelse Whitfield, age 5

Meandering Ribbons

Japanese silk ribbon can be used to decorate a fabric piece or wander over several. This ribbon is usually 4mm wide and is very soft and pliable; it handles almost like bias. It is available in a wide range of colors, too. Use this ribbon to create interesting patterns over the base work. The ribbon can be tacked in place with beads or French knots spaced close together to prevent the ribbon from snagging.

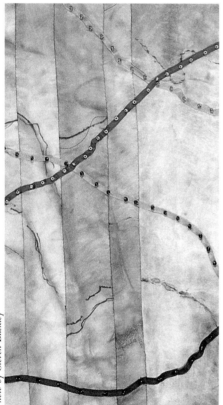

Photo by Steven Buckley

Silk dyed by author in an Yvonne Porcella class.

Ribbon Ruffles

Silk or organza ribbons make wonderful ruffles. Just run a gathering stitch down the center of the ribbon and pull the thread to gather. For a full ruffle, use double the length of ribbon. Even out the gathers and sew the ruffle to the base by hand. Ruffles can be highlighted with French knots or beads.

Ruth's Ruched Ribbon

Here is one of my favorite stitches taught to me by Ruth Stonely of Brisbane, Australia. Not only is she an internationally-known quilt artist, she is also a wonderful teacher. The ribbon can meander along crazy quilt seams and be worked in circles for flowers.

Photos by Judith Baker Montano

1. Thread a fine needle with a smooth metallic thread. Choose a long length of 4mm or wider silk ribbon.

2. Anchor the silk ribbon firmly to the fabric with the thread. Make a slip knot on the back side of the fabric and come back up with the metallic thread. Hold the ribbon in your free hand. Take large uneven running stitches in the middle of the ribbon. (Ruth insists that the sloppier the stitches, the better the ruching looks!) End with the needle under the ribbon. You should have 3" to 4" of running stitches.

3. Go into the fabric about ½" from the anchored end. Pull gently and the ribbon will gather up into the ½" space.

4. Come back up in the center of the ribbon and continue to make 3" to 4" of running stitches. Again, end under the ribbon and sew it ½" from point B. Use the point of the needle to arrange the gathers. Depending on the amount of running stitches and the width of the ribbon, the gathers can be very loose or tight.

5. For a fuller look and more contrast, try using two 4mm silk ribbons laid side by side. A second ribbon can be added into a single line of ruched ribbon. Simply anchor the second ribbon into the desired area and hold the two ribbons in your free hand.

6. Make sure they overlap just slightly on the inside edges. Now take large, uneven running stitches along those overlapped edges.

Twisted Ribbon

Twisted ribbon designs are pretty as fillers, and the ribbon can be tacked in place with beads or French knots. Choose a design (a bow, a zigzag, or a heart, for example) then cut the ribbon 1¾ times the length needed. Anchor one end of the ribbon in place with a bead or French knot. If you're trying to form a specific shape, lightly trace the shape onto the fabric, then follow the lines with the ribbon, twisting it at a right angle, alternating left, then right, as you go. Place a knot or bead to secure each twist. If the beads or knots are too far apart, the ribbon will snag.

Ribbon Prairie Points

Prairie points can be made with materials other than ribbon. They can be sewn directly into a seam or tucked under a lace edging, and decorated with beads or French knots. Use a ribbon at least ½" wide, cut twice the width to form a rectangle (A). Fold down the top corners to the center of the bottom edge to form a triangle (B). Press the triangle shape flat (C). The ribbon prairie point can be used on either side.

Gathered Flower

Small rosettes add a very delicate look to your work. Use narrow ribbon (½") cut about 3" long. Fold under one end and baste along one long edge (A). Gather tightly. Overlap the folded edge over the raw edge and stitch (B). If you use thread that matches the ribbon, you can use it to sew the rosette directly onto the fabric. Tack it only where the edges meet. Add beads or

Ribbons make fun, colorful embellishments on crazy quilt projects. On their own, or used with other embellishments, ribbons can cover seams or create a dimensional effect. This photo shows several ways to use ribbon. From upper left (clockwise), the techniques shown are: Gathered Flowers (highlighted with French knots and Lazy Daisy), a Twisted Ribbon bow (tacked with French knots), Meandering Ribbon (tacked with beads), Prairie Points, a large Concertina Rose with Ribbon Leaves, Embroidered Ribbon (with added button trim), Folded Ribbon Roses with Ribbon Leaves, and a Ruffled Ribbon.

French knots to the center along with the Lazy Daisy leaves.

Ribbon Leaves

To complement your ribbon or fabric roses, make leaves of ribbon, too. Cut a ribbon 1½ times its width and fold it like a prairie point (A). Gather the wide edge with a basting stitch (B), then tack the leaf in place under the rose.

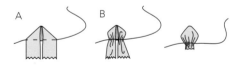

Concertina Rose

Using 3mm or 6mm ribbon, cut a length about 10" long. Thread a needle, using thread that matches the ribbon, and knot the end.

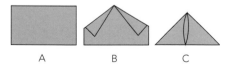

Fold the ribbon at a right angle in the center (A). Fold the horizontal section of the ribbon over and to the left.

Bring the ribbon up on the bottom and fold it up and over. The folds will take on a square look. Keep folding from right side to top to left side to bottom until the ribbon is used up (B).

Grasp the two ends in one hand and pull gently down on one end (it doesn't matter which one) until a rose is formed (C).

With the knotted thread, go down through the top and up again (do this two or three times). Finish on the bottom and wrap the base tightly. Make a slip knot and cut the thread, leaving a 6" tail, which will be used to sew the rose down later.

You can learn how to make the Folded Ribbon Rose pictured above in *The Art of Silk Ribbon Embroidery.*

These simple ribbon embroidery stitches will get you started. Once you've begun, you'll find it hard to stop!

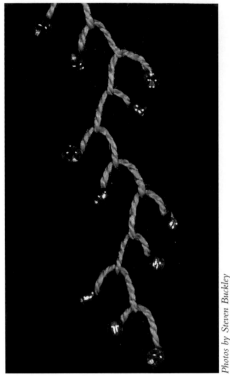

Beads provide the finishing touch at the ends of feather stitches

Antique beaded piece from author's collection

Beads

Good beads come in a wide variety of shapes, sizes, colors and finishes.

- Opaque beads give off a soft glow.
- Cut glass beads reflect light like crystal.
- Transparent beads sparkle.
- Luster seed beads have a metallic look.
- Iris beads have a deep, iridescent luster.

Needles & Thread

Beading needles come in a range of sizes and lengths. A long, thin needle is used only when the needle must be long enough to pick up many beads at a time. A shorter needle, called a sharp, is best for crazy quilting because you usually sew beads on one at a time.

The proper size of the needle depends on the size of the bead. The rule of thumb is to use the next highest number for the needle.

Use Nymo® thread by Belding Corticelli for all bead work. It is made just for beading and nothing else is as good.

Regular thread gives way over time and the beads will be lost. Nylon filament will stretch and the beads become loose. With Nymo thread, the bead is held firmly in place, with the bead sitting up on its side, where the most color shows.

Embroidery Highlights

When beads are used to accent embroidery, they are sewn on one at a time. Pour a few beads into a wide, shallow dish so they can be easily picked up with the needle. Tap or shake the plate so all the beads fall over onto their "hole side." Do not try to work with them from the storage container, as this can be very awkward and frustrating.

Bring the needle up at the point of the stitch, pick up a bead on the needle, then go back down into the fabric close to the same hole. Pull the thread with a bounce to lodge the bead securely on its side, and into the fabric. Go on to the next stitch, and do the same.

As a precaution, I like to tie a knot at the back of every fourth bead. This way, if a bead is pulled off, it won't start a chain reaction and the other beads will stay in place.

Use beads to highlight stitches such as the Feather stitch, Cretan, Herringbone and the Buttonhole. Use it in place of a French knot for a varied effect.

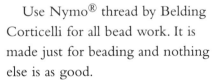

Sewn Beadwork

To make flower shapes with lines of beads, the beads are sewn on in rows, curves or circles. On a long beading needle, pick up as many beads as are needed for the line. Let them fall down the thread and into position on the fabric. Put the needle down through the fabric and come up at every third bead and couch between the beads.

Couch the beading thread after every third bead. Work the beading thread around to form the desired shape, couching as you go.

Example of Native American beadwork

Photo by Steven Buckley

Beaded pouch made by Kathy Miller, 1998; purchased by the author.

Knots and Other Things

I think the finishing touches are a major step in producing a professional, artistic project. For extra pizzazz, you might consider making knots and loops, instead of an ordinary button closure on garments. Cording finishes garments and accessories like nothing else. And tassels are fun decorations for garments, quilts, pillows, and other projects.

Chinese Button Balls

Chinese Button Balls

Loops and button balls, made of rat-tail cording, add a rich detail to crazy quilt garments. Button balls take a little practice to make, but the effect is worth the effort. Use about 6" of cording for each ball. Follow the illustration below to make as many knotted balls as desired, leaving at least a 1" tail to sew into the seam. Remember, the heavier the cording, the larger the button will be.

Knotted Loops

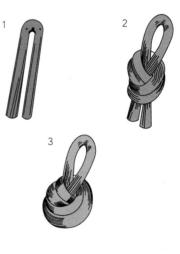

Loops make nice closures on many garments, with a knot or a button.

A 6" length of rat-tail cord makes a good size loop. Fold the cord in half (1) and tie a loose slipknot close to the open end (2), as illustrated. Manipulate the knot with your fingers to flatten it (3).

On most garments, loops and balls are sewn into a seam, but on some projects, this is impossible. When this is the case, tuck the loose ends of the cording under and tack the knot in place, using strong thread that is the same color as the cording.

Tassels

The Victorians loved tassels and used them generously on quilts and pillow corners. Tassels are great to hang off wall hangings or to decorate closures on garments. They are expensive to buy, but easy to make, in any size you like. There are many books out on the art of tassel making.

I like to make tassels with silk buttonhole twist. Use a piece of cardboard as wide as you want your tassel to be long; for example, use a 3" wide cardboard for a 3" long tassel. Wind the thread around the cardboard (1). The more thread you use, the fatter the tassel. Gather the thread at the top and tie (2) using a thread long enough that it will serve later to attach the tassel to the project. Clip the other end of the tassel and remove the cardboard. Now, wind a neck around the tied end (3) using matching thread. If necessary, tie a thread onto the end for attaching the tassel to the finished item.

A very simple tassel can be made from cotton floss. Take the whole skein and simply cut it in half (keep the little paper holders at each end). Now wrap the folded ends and attach to your work.

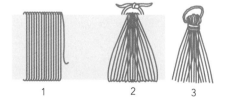

    1   2   3

Buttons

Buttons are a quick, easy source of color, shape and texture. They can be ceramic, shell, mother-of-pearl, bone, leather, metal or plastic, or covered with complementary fabric. Buttons can add a touch of whimsy to crazy quilting. They can march along in neat rows or bunch up in interesting clusters. Buttons can accent a ribbon, or hold a bow in place.

Look for buttons in antique shops, garage sales, and estate sales, as well as traditional fabric and button shops. I don't mind spending more for antique buttons, if they are just the right touch to finish off a project. Antique pearl buttons are such a pretty touch for crazy quilting.

Used in rows, tiny pearl baby buttons are especially effective. They almost look like flowers if you sew them on with yellow silk thread and edge them with green Lazy Daisy stitches.

To make a paisley shape, start out with a large, flat button and rotate outward, decreasing the button size, to achieve the desired shape. Ball buttons make nice clusters, especially in a mix of sizes and colors.

Sew buttons onto the basework with silk buttonhole twist, using a complementary color, or use Nymo thread, and add beads as you sew the button on. This forms visual interest.

Treat the use of buttons like lace. If the buttons are very old and valuable, put them on projects that will get little handling. If an antique button will finish off a clothing project, then use it, but make sure it's sewn on securely and tie double knots on the back. If a project is washable, use buttons that can stand up to repeated cleaning and use.

Laces, Doilies, and Hankies

Lace acts as an element of texture and design in crazy quilting. By laying lace or a doily over a deep, rich color, you add an element of drama.

Use long, narrow pieces of lace to break up large pieces, or to create curved lines. I use a glue stick to hold the lace in place. After I decide on a pleasing design, I tack them into place using my Nymo thread, with an appliqué stitch. Lace can be highlighted with ribbon or embroidery stitches, too. Add beads or small buttons for sparkle. Colored lace can carry through a color scheme. White or off-white lace, applied to a pastel fabric, takes on a muted, softer look. Keep lace embellishments in the same mood as the rest of the work.

Ruffled lace adds a soft, feminine look to crazy quilt projects. When using lace, keep in mind how much wear and tear a finished project will receive. The price and/or sentimental value will determine if you can cut into it.

Cleaning Antique Lace

Old lace, doilies and hankies are often soiled and stained and must be cleaned carefully before they can be used.

Try washing stained lace by hand in mild detergent.

Wrap it in a towel and squeeze out excess water, then let the lace dry flat. If stains persist, diluted laundry bleach might work on tough stains, but it must be rinsed very thoroughly, and the lace washed after bleaching.

If all efforts to clean a stain fail, try cutting away the stained parts, or let the stain dictate the look, and tea dye the entire piece.

Coloring Lace

Tea

Light-colored laces and fabrics, steeped in tea, take on a patina of age that is charming. Different varieties of tea give off a different color from rose to peach.

To make the tea solution, boil a kettle of water with four tea bags in it for 15 minutes. Strain the solution and return it to simmer. Then put the lace into the simmering tea. When the lace has simmered for 15 minutes, take it out and put it in a setting solution of ½ cup white vinegar to three cups of water. Let it set for 15 minutes, then rinse it thoroughly and press.

Coffee

I use instant coffee and boiling water to create an antique patina on lace, fabric and ribbons.

The more teaspoons of coffee you use, the darker the effect. Soak the materials in the coffee mixture for 10-15 minutes. Rinse under water, and dry.

Gentian Violet

My friends in Australia use a product called Conte Crystals to produce a deep golden shade to their laces and fabrics. Once again, the

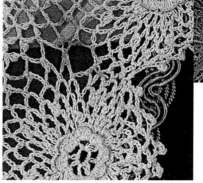

stronger the solution and the longer it soaks, the deeper the tint.

In America, Conte Crystals are known as Gentian Violet, and can be obtained in crystal form over the counter from the local pharmacist.

Boil a quart of water. In a Pyrex bowl, dissolve three to four teaspoons of Gentian Violet crystals in the hot water. It will turn a bright fuchsia-violet. Soak the materials. The solution will turn to a brownish-gold as it cools. Rinse thoroughly after the dye-bath, and dry.

Doilies

Small doilies can be used whole or cut into fan shapes for spectacular effects. These pieces—round, oval, rectangle or square—add a wonderful element of shape, texture and color to the work. A doily covers a multitude of sins if your seams aren't quite perfect.

Hankies

Handkerchiefs, especially old ones, can be a wonderful design source. Many old hankies have beautiful tatted and crocheted edges, or fancy embroidered initials. Some have four decorated corners that make great triangular overlays. Hankies generally add a soft, feminine touch, as well as a feeling of old-fashioned elegance.

Crazy Quilt, c 1860, United States
Denver Art Museum Collection: Gift from Mr. and Mrs. Robert A. Young, 1984.342
© *Denver Art Museum 2001*

"Victorian Melody" by Judith Baker Montano. Courtesy of Del Ellis

Photo by A&I Photography

Projects

Now it's time to put our theories into practice. The following pages feature full-sized patterns and step-by-step directions for 12 crazy quilt projects. Use these projects to gain experience with crazy quilt techniques and confidence in your design ability. Then branch out to design projects of your own— holiday decorations, tablecloths, full-size quilts, etc.

YARDAGES GIVEN ARE BASED ON 44/45" WIDE FABRICS.

Needlecase Pocket

A fast and lovely project, this needlecase is very useful for anyone who sews. It is large enough to hold embroidery scissors, thread, needles and a thimble. With a hanging cord, it can be worn around your neck for your sewing needs or can act as a pouch. Without the cord, it can be used in a sewing basket or attached to a belt as a decorative pocket.

Finished size 4" x 4½"

Materials Needed

Fabrics

- Small scraps of 6 to 8 fancy fabrics (mix of solids, textures, and prints)
- 8" square of pre-washed muslin
- 4" square of felt
- 6" x 18" moiré or low-nap velvet for lining and backing

Other Materials

- 7" x 14" fleece or needle-punch batting
- Embroidery floss or silk buttonhole twist in several colors
- Nymo thread, beading needle, and beads
- 4½" grosgrain ribbon (¼" wide)
- 74" rat-tail cord
- Snaps or Velcro® circles for closure
- Plastic for window template

1. This piece is an exercise in the Centerpiece Method described on page 22. On 5" x 5½" muslin piece, place a five-sided piece of dark fabric at the center. Working clockwise, sew down each rectangle fabric piece in turn; after all the angles are covered, cut shapes and sizes. Keep the pieces small and irregularly shaped.

2. When the base piece is filled with crazy quilting, use a plastic window template to find a 4½" x 5" area. Mark this rectangle on the fabric with water-erasable pen, then cut away the excess.

3. Cover each seam with embroidery stitches (see Stitch Dictionary, page 63.) Add special embellishments, such as embroidered initials, spiderwebs, beads, or buttons. This is a great way to personalize gifts for any recipient. Usually, the centerpiece is a good place to add such a highlight.

4. Cut two 4½" x 5" rectangles from the fleece. Cut three rectangles from the lining/backing fabric. Cut the felt 1" smaller all around, 2½" x 3", using pinking shears for a nice edge.

5. Glue or tack the felt piece to the right side of one lining rectangle. On the right side of the other lining piece, add the grosgrain ribbon. Position the ribbon 1½" from the top edge, and stitch it down at the ends (overlap 1" on either side of center). This will be your scissors holder.

6. Lay the lining piece down, ribbon side up. Put the finished front piece over it, matching right sides together. Finally, lay a piece of fleece on top. Put one pin in each side to hold the layers together as you work.

7. Using a ¼" seam allowance, machine stitch all around; leave a 2" opening in the center of one end for turning.

8. Trim the fleece ⅛" from the seam to reduce bulk. Turn right side out and whipstitch the opening closed.

9. Repeat the process for the back of the needlecase, layering the remaining backing piece (right side up) with the lining (felt side down) and the remaining fleece. Press both finished sections.

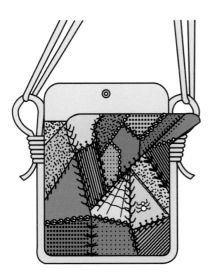

10. Whipstitch the two sections together, up to the designated line 1½" from the top edge.

11. Cut 14" of rat-tail cord for the edging. Fold over a small loop at one end of the cord and hold it in place at the needlecase edge as illustrated above. With contrasting floss or buttonhole twist, wrap the loop in place.

12. Use remaining rat-tail to make a neck cord. Sew on snaps or Velcro circles at center top.

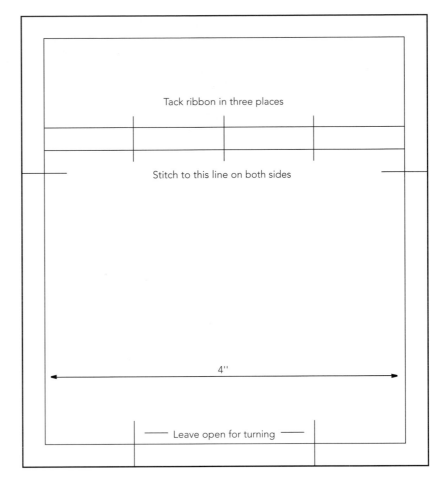

Tack ribbon in three places

Stitch to this line on both sides

4"

Leave open for turning

Heart Bag

We often wish we could leave our big purses behind. Here is an elegant answer. This heart bag is just big enough to hold a change purse, lipstick, compact and a small comb. It is pretty enough to double as a large pendant, if desired. It can also be adapted to a belt pocket or needlecase. The technique can be applied to any size or shape of pattern.

Finished size 4" x 6"

Materials Needed

Fabrics

- Small scraps of 10 to 12 fancy fabrics (solids, textures, and prints)
- 9" square of pre-washed muslin
- ¼ yard heavy moiré or satin for lining and backing *

Other Materials

- 9" x 16" fleece or needle-punch batting
- Embroidery floss or silk buttonhole twist
- Nymo thread, beading needle, and beads
- Two pieces (different colors) rat-tail cord, each 45" long
- 9" square of template plastic *(optional)*
- Water-erasable pen
- Snaps or Velcro circles for closure

* These instructions are for a solid fabric back. If you prefer, you can make a reversible bag by making two crazy quilt hearts.

1. Center the five-sided centerpiece on the muslin square. Using the Centerpiece Method (see page 22), sew on rectangle pieces of fabric, working clockwise. Cut angles and shapes until the square is filled.

2. Position the template plastic over the heart pattern on page 43. Trace the outer heart shape onto the plastic. Using small scissors or an art knife, cut out the heart window.

3. Lay the window template on the crazy quilting. Move it around until you find a design placement that you like. Mark the outline of the heart on the fabric with the water-erasable pen. Cut away excess fabric on this marked line.

4. Cover each seam with embroidery stitches. (See Stitch Dictionary, page 63.) Add initials, spiders and webs, flowers or other motifs. Highlight the stitches with beads. Add other embellishments as desired.

5. From the lining/backing fabric, cut three hearts, using your window template to mark the shape on the fabric. Cut two hearts of fleece.

6. Put one lining heart on top of the crazy quilted heart, right sides together and matching all edges. Place one fleece heart on top of the lining. Machine stitch all around, taking a ¼" seam allowance. Leave a 2" opening on one side as indicated on the pattern.

7. Clip curves and points of the seam allowance, up to the stitching line. Trim fleece to ⅛" from seam. Turn heart right-side out; press it flat. Close the opening by hand.

8. Make the back of the heart bag in the same fashion, using the two remaining hearts of lining/backing and the fleece. When done, you'll have two finished hearts the same size. Press them carefully.

9. Whipstitch the edges of the two hearts together, up to the line designated on the pattern (1½" from top).

10. Twist the two cord pieces together. Tack the cord in place. It can be adjusted to your desired length one of two ways:

A. Position the center of the cord on your neck or shoulder, letting the cord hang down. At the desired height, pin the cord to both sides of the bag at the point where the two hearts join. Using but-tonhole twist, whip the cord to the bag down to the point. Make a small knot in the cord at the point. You can cut away the extra cord or let it dangle loose.

¼" seam allowance

Cut template on this line

Whipstitch to this line on both sides

Leave open for turning

Seam line

Cutting line

Or

B. Fold the twisted cord in half to find the center. Position the center point of the cord at the bottom point of the heart. Using buttonhole twist, whip the cording onto both sides of the heart up to the point at which back and front separate.

Keeping the cords twisted together, tie a knot at the top.

For either method, sew extra wraps around the cord at the top of each side where it will take the most stress.

Photo by Judith Baker Montano

Weeping Heart Needlecase

A beautiful, soft=sided needlecase that looks small and delicate, but holds lots of needles. This case can be added to a chatelaine or can be attached to a sewing basket.

Materials Needed

- Two 9" squares of template plastic
- Seven fancy fabrics
- 12" square of fancy fabric for backing, lining, and heart insert
- 6" square of muslin
- 8" square fleece
- Silk ribbon, embroidery threads, Nymo thread, beads, #10 sharps needle, buttons, doodads
- 12" trim for edging, or 30" of 4mm silk ribbon for ruched edging
- Water-erasable pen

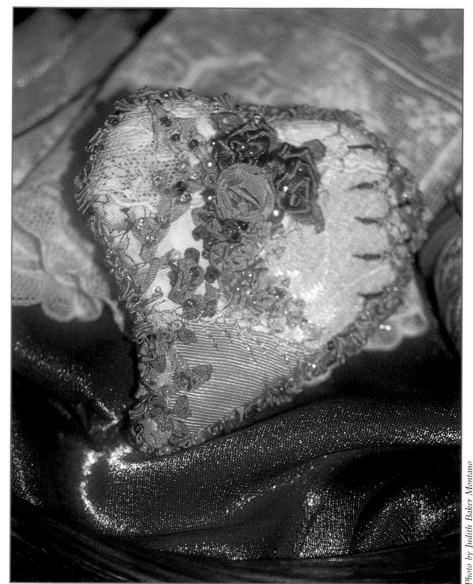

Photo by Judith Baker Montano

Photo by Judith Baker Montano

1. Trace one heart shape on the outer line onto the template plastic. Cut two linings and one backing. Cut two fleece.

2. Trace a second heart of the inner dotted line on template plastic, adding a ¼" seam allowance. Cut two fancy fabrics for the needle insert.

3. Using the Centerpiece Method, (See page 22.) fill in the 6" square of muslin.

4. Lay the window heart template with the ¼" seam line down on the crazy quilt square. Arrange until you have a pleasing design. Mark with the water-erasable pen and cut out.

5. Now embroider and embellish the crazy quilt heart.

6. Put the crazy quilt heart on top of one lining heart, right sides together, and one fleece heart on top. Put one pin in each side to hold the layers together as you work.

7. With a ½" seam allowance, machine stitch all around. Leave a 2" opening at the center of one side.

Photo by Judith Baker Montano

8. Trim the fleece ⅛" from the seam to reduce bulk. Turn and hand sew the opening closed.

9. Repeat for the back of the needlecase. Press both finished sections.

10. Lay small heart insert pieces right sides together. Sew a ¼" seam around the pieces, but leave a 1" opening. Trim seams to ⅛", then turn. Sew opening closed, and press.

11. Insert this piece between the two larger hearts, then whip-stitch the three pieces together at the hinge mark.

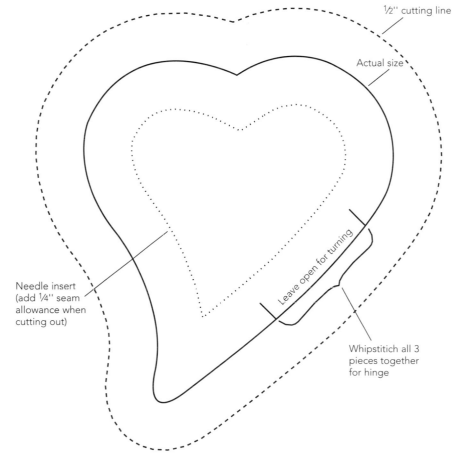

½'' cutting line

Actual size

Needle insert (add ¼'' seam allowance when cutting out)

Leave open for turning

Whipstitich all 3 pieces together for hinge

Heart Pendant

You can make heart pendants in complementary colors to set off any outfit. When you've made one, chances are you'll want to make more! It's a perfect gift and a beautiful ornament that always attracts notice. Embroidered initials make each pendant uniquely personal.

Photo by Alan Carter

Materials Needed

Fabrics

- Small scraps of 5 to 8 fancy fabrics for crazy quilting (solids, textures, and prints)
- Two 5" squares of muslin
- 8" square of dark (black) cotton for embroidered center
- 5" square of leather backing

Other Materials

- 5" x 15" fleece or needle-punch batting
- 31" rat-tail cord for neckcord
- 12" rat-tail cord (another color) for edging
- Fabric glue
- Embroidery floss or silk buttonhole twist
- Darning needle and strong thread
- 5" square of heavy artboard (Crescent Board 200 weight)
- Nymo thread, beading needle and beads
- Buttons and doodads
- Ribbon, lace, or trims
- Punchneedle, #1 or #3 (optional)

- Water-erasable marker
- 8" square of template plastic

1. Trace the heart shape template (page 79) onto a 4¼" x 4½" piece of template plastic and cut out the heart shape. Use the template to mark the heart shape on your materials. Cut one heart of muslin, three of fleece, one of artboard and one of leather. No seam allowances need to be added.

2. Trace a flower or other embroidery design onto the square of dark cotton. First work the outlines of the shape in either punchneedle or other embroidery, then fill in.

3. Cut out the finished design with enough fabric around it to cut five angles for the centerpiece.

4. The remaining muslin square is the base for the crazy quilting. Position the embellished center on it, and begin sewing down small fabric rectangles. (See Centerpiece Method, page 22.) Work around, clockwise, until the square is filled in. Press the completed square.

5. Lay the heart template on the crazy quilting and move it around until you find a design placement that you like. Mark the heart shape on the fabric with the water-erasable pen. Measure out ½" all around the heart outline, as illustrated, then cut out on the outer line. You need the extra fabric for sewing it to the back.

6. Outline each seam with decorative stitches. (See Stitch Dictionary, page 63.) Finish off the stitches with beads, French knots or other decorative details.

7. Stack all the cut hearts in order, from the bottom: muslin, artboard, three fleece, and on top, the crazy quilt heart (this is larger than the others.)

8. With a darning needle and strong thread, whipstitch the crazy quilt heart over the fleece and artboard, using the bottom muslin as an anchor. Sew around twice; on the second round, stitch deeper into the muslin to pull the assembly taut and even.

9. Cut the rat-tail for the neck cord to a length you like. Tie a slipknot at both ends, leaving a ½" tail.

10. Glue leather backing to heart. Let some glue ooze out of the seam. While the glue is still wet, insert the tails of the neck cord between heart and leather, measuring out ½" to either side of the heart center. Hold tight until the glue dries.

11. Add cord around the heart edges, starting at the center top. (The glue that oozed out will hold it in place.) Whipstitch the cord down with buttonhole twist.

Heart Belt

This belt is made of two crazy quilt hearts, centered on a silk tie-belt. It is most effective and elegant, just the accent you need for a special outfit. The belt ties in the back, so it is adjustable to any waist size. The ends can be tucked in under the belt or left hanging down.

Materials Needed

Hearts

Use the materials list on page 46 and the heart shape template on page 79 for the Heart Pendant. You will need enough materials to make two hearts. You need only 12" of rat-tail to edge each heart.

Belt

- ¼ yard silk or comparable fabric
- ¼ yard cotton (same color as silk)
- Matching thread for top stitching
- ¼ to 1 yard belting or buckram (2½" wide)

1. Make two hearts as described on page 46.

2. Measure your waist. Cut the stiff belting 5" shorter than the waist measurement. Cut the silk and cotton pieces 15" longer than the waist measurement, 5½" wide.

3. Lay the two fabric pieces right sides together, and match all edges. On the two short ends only, machine stitch ¼" from the edge. Turn the belt right side out through one of the open sides. This gives you a clean finished end for the tie-belt.

4. Lay the belt flat, cotton side up. Center the belting on top. Now fold the fabric over the belting so that it meets at the center. Whipstitch the fabric edges together by folding one edge over the other. Do not sew through the belting. Finish out to both ends.

5. Machine top stitch through all layers at both edges and the center. Add additional top-stitching as desired.

6. Fold the belt in half and mark the center. Glue the hearts in place as shown. Weight down the hearts until the glue is completely dry.

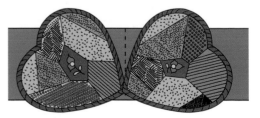

Oval Needlecase

This hinged needlecase looks a bit like a delectable Easter egg. You can't stop after making just one. These cases also are wonderful gifts.

Materials Needed

For Landscape with Tree Needlecase
- Sky fabric
- Five fabrics for landscape pieces

All other ingredients are the same
- Small scraps of 6 to 8 fancy fabrics
- Two 6" squares of muslin
- 10" square of heavy artboard (Crescent board 200 weight)
- 12" square of fancy fabric for lining and backing
- 12" square heavy 1½"-wide velvet ribbon (for needles)
- 12" satin ribbon (for ties and hinge)
- 6" x 15" fleece or needle-punch batting
- 18" fancy cording for edging
- 5" x 7" rectangle of template plastic
- Fabric glue
- Embroidery threads, beads, lace
- Darning needle and strong thread
- Water-erasable pen

1. Make two plastic templates for the oval, using the pattern on page 79. Make one template for actual size line and another for cutting line.

2. Using the actual size line, cut 4 art boards and 1 fleece. Using the cutting line, cut 1 fleece, 1 muslin, 3 fancy fabrics (2 for liners, and 1 backing).

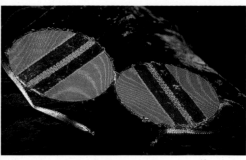

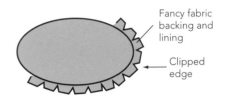

Photos by Judith Baker Montano

3. Select the landscape design you wish to make or use the illustration on page 79. Fill in the remaining muslin square.

4. Using the cutting line oval template cut the oval shape.

5. Outline each seam with embroidery stitches. Highlight the stitches with beads.

6. Stack all the ovals together, starting with the muslin oval on the bottom. Then add the artboard, 2 fleece (one cut on actual line, the next on the cutting line), and the finished oval on top.

7. Turn over. With a darning needle and strong thread, whipstitch the finished oval over the fleece and artboard, using the bottom muslin as an anchor. Sew around twice; on the second round, stitch deeper into the muslin to pull the assembly taut and even.

8. Spread glue (or use spray adhesive) on one side of the artboard back. Lay fancy backing fabric, wrong side down, onto the glued area. Clip the seam allowances (fold to the back and glue in place).

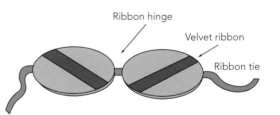

Fancy fabric backing and lining

Clipped edge

9. Repeat this process with the two lining ovals. Lay the velvet ribbon in place. Glue edges to the back.

10. Glue the front finished side to the liner. Insert the 5" tie ribbon and 2" hinge ribbon.

Ribbon hinge

Velvet ribbon

Ribbon tie

11. Glue the fabric backing piece and the liner piece together. Insert the 5" ribbon tie. Now insert the ribbon hinge. (Leave a ⅛" space so it will lie flat when closed. Make sure the velvet ribbon forms a "V" shape when open.)

12. Lay a bead of glue along the joined edges and cover with fancy braid. Tuck the raw edges in-between the two halves.

Crazy Quilt Painting

Crazy quilt paintings mix old with new, almost like painting with fabric to create a mood or a scene. With just the change of color or texture, each painting takes on a new and different look. This crazy quilt painting is done with pattern pieces laid down string-quilting style, then embellished with Victorian stitches and beads. It is usually best to keep to a two-color scheme (such as teal and rose, or peach and blue). Use shades of the two colors, mixing in a variety of texture and pattern.

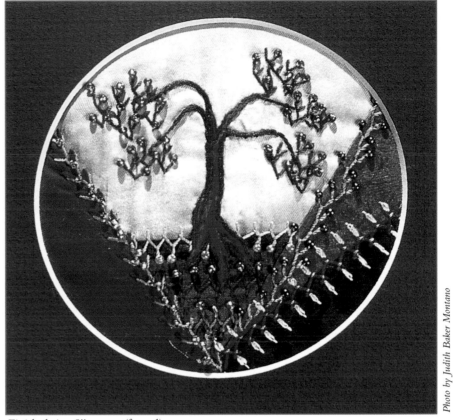

Finished size 8" square (framed)

Materials Needed

Fabrics

- Small scraps appropriate for the scene, including sky blue
- 8" square of pre-washed muslin

Other Materials

- 6" square of fleece or needle-punch batting
- Embroidery floss or silk buttonhole twist
- 8" square cardboard or artboard
- Nymo thread, beading needle and beads
- White marking pencil or water-erasable pen
- Glue
- Masking tape
- 6" square of template plastic for window plus additional plastic for pattern templates
- 8" square of mat board with 4" circle cut out★
- 8" square frame★

★Many stores sell precut mats and easy-to-assemble frames. If you can't find what you want, go to a regular frame store, but be prepared to pay a higher price for custom-made items. For a more economical way, look in your Yellow Pages for a "do-it-yourself" frame shop. In this kind of store, you select materials that are cut for you, and the shop staff will help you to assemble the frame yourself.

1. Use the 4" circle in the mat board to make a plastic window template.

2. Trace the pattern in the center of the 8" muslin square. Then, mark a second, outer circle, ½" larger all around.

3. You can make any scene by cutting fabric pieces by hand as you go, or you can make a template for the pattern pieces. The patterns given include seam allowances as indicated (¼" on inside seams and ½" on the outside edges).

4. Sew the pieces down in numerical order, sewing on the marked lines. Press each piece flat before adding the next. If the pattern lines are covered by another fabric, mark guidelines on the top fabric.

5. When all pieces are sewn and pressed, lay the window template over the piece. Mark the 4" circle with white pencil or water-erasable pen.

6. Sketch in a free-form tree, using water-erasable pen. (Just a splash of cold water later will remove any telltale marks.) Use embroidery floss or silk buttonhole twist to make a tree trunk of Stem

Crazy Quilt Painting Patterns—Sunrise Scene

5 Pattern Pieces

¼" seam allowances on inside seams

½" seam allowances on outside edges

Arrows indicate fabric grain lines

stitches. Use the Feather stitch to make twigs and leaves. (See Stitch Dictionary, page 68.)

7. Cover the seams with embroidery stitches. Add beads to highlight the stitches.

8. Center the finished picture in the mat opening. Pull the fabric tight behind the circle opening. Tape it to the back of the mat with masking tape.

9. Cut out a 4" circle of fleece. With the picture lying face down, lay the fleece circle on the back of the picture.

10. Lay a bead of glue around the back of the mat. Press the cardboard square on top, wedging the fleece between the cardboard and the picture. (The fleece puffs out the fabric scene in the mat opening, giving it a rounded look.) Weight down the edges (not the center) of the mat until the glue is completely dry. Then, just pop the picture into a frame for unique fabric art.

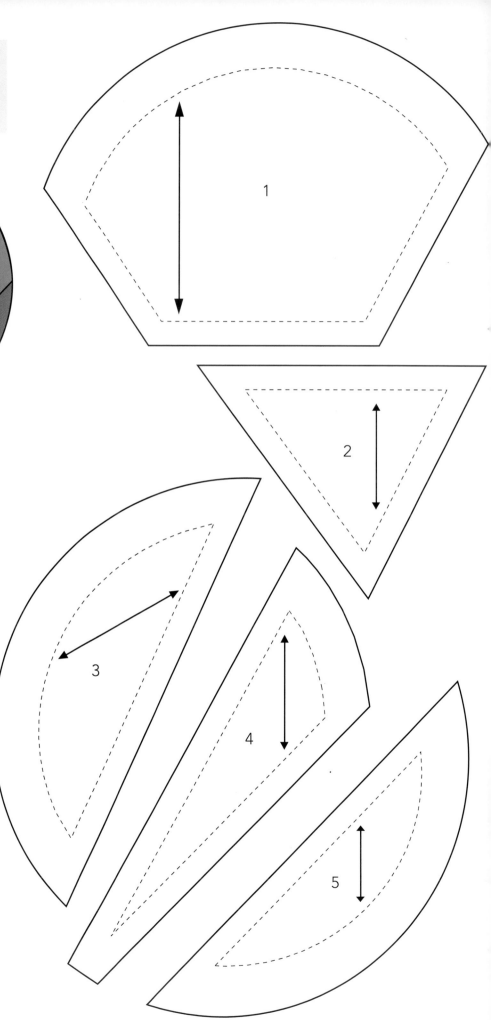

Chicken Bumble Pin Cushion

Photo by Judith Baker Montano

A bumble was originally a Victorian toy made for babies. I was gifted with a crazy-quilt bumble in Australia, and fell in love with it. Later I saw a rooster bumble made with quilted squares—and then made one for my friend Phyl Drew. They are so much fun to make.

Materials Needed

- Two 5" squares of muslin
- Eight fancy fabrics—solids, textures and prints
- One 4½" x 4½" square of fancy fabric (for tail)
- One 3½" x 3½" square of fancy fabric (for tail)
- One 4" square of red fabric for wattle and comb
- One 2" square of gold fabric for beak
- Polyester fiber fill
- Two black beads for eyes
- Embroidery threads
- Nymo thread, beading needles, and beads

1. Fill in the two 5" squares of muslin with crazy quilting; keep the pieces small.

2. Embroider and embellish both squares. Add beads if desired. Set aside.

3. Now fold the first tail square (4½" x 4½") into a prairie point, and press.

4. Fold second tail square (3½" x 3½") into a prairie point and press. Pin on top of first prairie point as shown.

5. Cut two red wattles and two red combs. Sew along the sew line. Turn out and press. Pin in place on one crazy quilt square.

6. Fold gold 2" square into a prairie point and fold again. Pin in place (in the beak area), folded side up.

How-to photos by Steven Buckley

Pin the three pieces (wattle, comb and beak) in the designated areas.

7. Lay the second crazy quilt square face down (right sides together). Sew on designated sides 1, 2, and 3.

8. Match up the seam lines of side 1 and side 3. Press down to form a center fold on each side.

Pin in the tail piece and sew to top piece of fabric. Now sew the sides 1" at each fold side.

9. Turn inside out. Stuff with polyester batting. Close the opening with hand stitching.

10. Sew eyes in place. Sew one bead on and through to the other side. Pull in a bit to create an indentation.

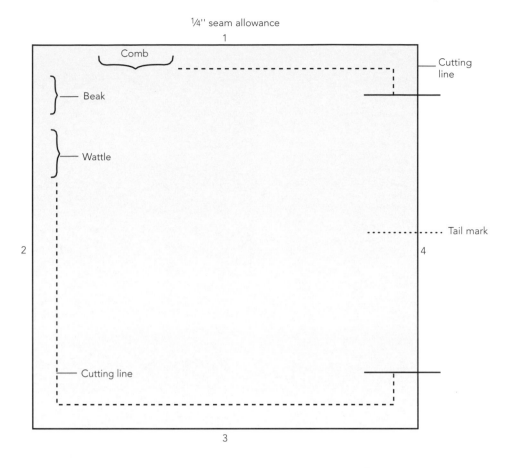

¼" seam allowance

1

Comb

Beak

Wattle

2

Cutting line

Tail mark

4

Cutting line

3

How-to photos by Steven Buckley

BEAK

⅛" seam allowance

COMB

Cut 2

⅛" seam allowance

WATTLE

Cut 1

Sabre Pouch

This elegant purse is comfortable at any occasion, be it afternoon tea, a wedding, or an evening at the opera. If the wedding is a very special one, the purse can be made to complement the bride's colors and given to her as a loving and lasting memento.

Materials Needed

- Nymo beading thread, beads, #10 sharps beading needle
- Embroidery, chenille, and tapestry needles
- Sharp scissors for fabric and embroidery work
- 6" embroidery hoop
- 10" square of template plastic
- Cording for drawstring—2 pieces 15" long for hand-held; or 32" for shoulder strap
- ¼ yard iron-on interfacing
- One tassel for bottom of purse

Option 1 for Crazy-Quilt Purse

- 12" x 15" rectangle of muslin (for 2 crazy quilt panels)
- ¼ yard of fancy fabric (silk) for two plain panels, and lining
- Eight 7" squares of fancy fabrics (a mix of three solids, three patterns, and two textures.)
- 3 fancy ribbons
- 2 pieces of lace and fancy trim
- A variety of embroidery threads (cotton, silk and metallics)
- Variety of Mokuba® Azlon ribbons
- Buttons and doodads

Option 2 for Plain Panels with Silk Ribbon Embroidery

- ¼ yard silk or fancy fabric for 2 panels and lining
- 15" of 3 assorted colors Kanagawa® silk buttonhole twist thread
- 15" of ⅜"-wide satin ribbon (may be silk or organza)
- Azlon Ribbon (4 greens, 2 purples)
- 7mm Azlon Ribbon (2 peaches)
- Variegated ribbon

1. Trace 2 outlines of panel onto the muslin and cut out ¼" beyond the line. Cut out plastic window template on cutting line. Trace and cut 2 interfacing panels using window template.

2. Work the crazy quilt pieces, filling in the whole panel. Iron flat (use spray starch on the back).

3. Lay the window template down on the finished panel and trace the cutting line. Then cut on this line. Iron interfacing to back of work.

4. Cut out the lining panels. Lay the lining right-sides together on the crazy quilt panel. Sew a ¼" seam. Trim seam to ¹⁄₁₆".

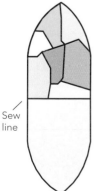

Sew line

Seam line or fold line for drawstring (casing) →

← Cutting line

← Cut out 2 outside panels and 2 lining panels. Includes ¼'' seam allowance.

.... Actual line

5. Lay right sides together of the two attached pieces (outside and liner) one on top of the other. Sew ¼" seam along the outside panels. Leave a ½" space at fold line for the cording. Leave a 3" space on one side of the lining.

— Crazy quilt panel

½'' space

½'' space

3" opening on lining

— Lining

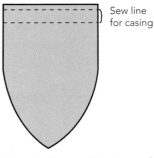

6. Reach into the space on the lining and pull the piece inside out. Press well. Sew the lining space closed. Now push the liner into the outside panel. Press or sew along top fold. Sew casing line.

Sew line for casing

7. Thread the cording into the casing. Add tassel.

Heirloom Collage

Create a beautiful heirloom using the Centerpiece method. Add crazy quilting to surround a family photo. May be framed as an 8" x 10" collage, or can be pieced together to form a wallhanging or small quilt.

Photo by Judith Baker Montano

Materials Needed

- 9" x 11" rectangle of muslin fabric
- 12 pieces of fancy fabric
- Silk fabric with photo transfer for center piece
- Lace, ribbons, fancy trims
- Buttons, beads and doodads
- Nymo thread, beading needle
- Silk ribbons, embroidery threads
- Two 8" x 6" fleece and one 8" x 10" mat

1. Cut the fabric with the photo transfer into a five-sided center piece. Proceed to fill in the muslin with the Center-piece Method. (See page 22.)

2. Add lace, ribbon, and trims.

3. Add Victorian stitches to every seam.

4. Add silk ribbon embroidery to highlight photograph if desired.

5. Add beads, buttons and doodads.

6. Refer to *Floral Stitches* (See Bibliography) for framing techniques using fleece and mat.

For Wallhanging or Quilt

1. Make the desired amount of rectangles.

2. Sew the rectangles together with ¼" seams. Press open the seams.

3. Add borders if desired.

You may want to make your quilt appear as an over-all crazy quilt piece. If so, refer to pages 20 and 26 for more information about the Overlapping technique for hiding seam lines.

Photo by A&I Photography

Victorian Pillow

This sweet little boudoir pillow can be made into a shower gift, ring-bearer's pillow, or christening gift. Color choices and ruffle materials can change the look dramatically. For an antique Victorian look, choose colors from the dark, dusty palette.

Materials Needed

Fabrics

- 14" square of muslin
- ⅓ yard cotton muslin for insert
- 12 pieces of fancy fabrics (mix of solids, texture, prints)
- 14" square for backing

Other Materials

- 4" x 14" rectangle of template plastic
- Small bag polyester batting
- 40" of ruffled lace—or 80" of flat lace or fabric for a double ruffle
- Laces, ribbons, trims
- Buttons, beads, doodads
- Embroidery threads, silk ribbons
- Beading thread and beading needle

1. Cut the half-heart shape out of template plastic. Since this becomes a permanent pattern, mark all directions on the plastic.

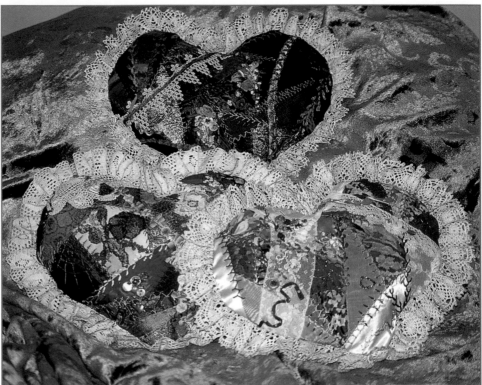

Finished size 12" x 10" (30cm x 25cm)

2. Draw two hearts of muslin and one heart of backing fabric on the cutting line. Set aside the muslin hearts for the pillow insert.

3. Cut a third muslin heart, ½" larger than the cutting line. Proceed to fill in with crazy quilting.

Assembly for Pillow:

1. Pin the lace or fabric ruffle in place, then baste by machine or hand onto the front of the finished piece. Pin the ruffle down so it stays in out of the way.

2. Lay the backing face down onto the ruffled crazy quilt piece. Pin together. Sew a ¼" seam, leaving a 3½" opening for the heart pillow insert. Remove pins, turn right side out and then remove the ruffle pins.

3. Sew the 2 muslin hearts together, but leave a 2" opening, then turn right side out. Stuff with batting.

4. Sew the opening closed. Then insert the muslin pillow into the 3½" opening of the fancy embroidered pillow.

5. Sew the 3½" opening closed with matching thread.

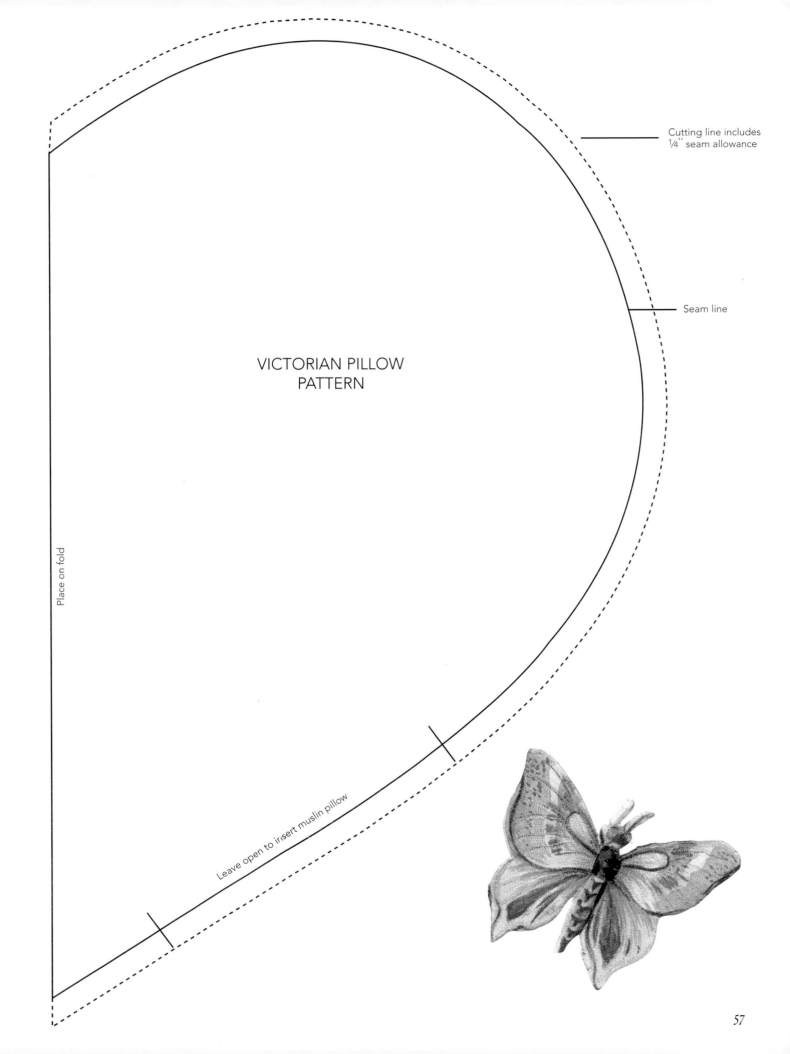

Cutting line includes ¼" seam allowance

Seam line

VICTORIAN PILLOW
PATTERN

Place on fold

Leave open to insert muslin pillow

Fancy Crazy Quilt Wallhanging

This wallhanging is a good intermediate piece. It is a larger project that incorporates the many lessons and challenges of crazy quilting. Victorian fans, used in each corner, give a nice feeling of balance and symmetry. These are pieced and added after the base crazy quilting is done. The center medallion shown is a crazy quilt landscape. The medallion can also be used to highlight a special piece of embroidery or memento. To make this project even easier, you can omit the medallion and make an overall design. Work with a color scheme in mind. You can use fancy fabrics or create a completely different look with "homey" fabrics such as wool, cotton and suede cloth.

Finished size 28½" x 38½"

Materials Needed

Fabrics

- Scraps of at least 12 different fancy fabrics for basework (silk, velvet, moiré, chintz, etc.) in a mixture of solids, textures and prints
- 1 yard pre-washed muslin for basework
- ⅞ yard for backing (add ¼ yard for a hanging sleeve)
- ½ yard for borders (satin, velvet or moiré)
- ⅜ yard for binding

Other Materials

- Embroidery floss or silk buttonhole twist
- Nymo thread, beading needle and beads
- Assorted lace, ribbon, and trims
- Buttons and doodads
- Metallic threads, if desired
- 24" of string and a pencil

1. Cut or tear the prewashed muslin to 22" x 32". This will be the base piece and it allows for ½" of extra fabric all around.

2. Tie one end of the string to the pencil to serve as a makeshift compass. Mark the string 9" from the pencil and again at 16" from the pencil.

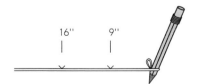

3. Grasp the string at the 9" mark and hold it at one corner of the muslin. Swing the pencil out and mark an arc on the muslin. Repeat at each corner to outline the positions of the fans. Now position the 16" mark at each corner to make large swinging lines as shown. These outline the center medallion.

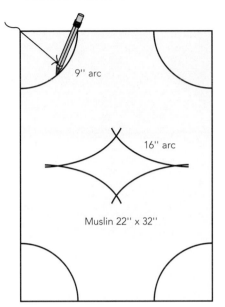

4. Cut borders before you sew. Cut two border strips 4¼" x 31" and two strips 4¼" x 41". The remaining border fabric can now be used in the basework.

5. Make the center medallion separate from the base piece. Copy the shape onto another piece of muslin, adding ½" for seam allowances all around. Fill in the medallion with a scene (as shown) or a motif of your choice.

6. Make 4 corner fans in the same way, separate from the muslin base. (Use the fan pattern on page 60.) Each fan has 4 segments, sewn together. Press under a ¼" seam allowance on the curved edge of each completed fan. Set aside.

7. Fill in the base piece with crazy quilting. Let the edges of the fabric pieces overlap slightly with the areas outlined for the medallion and fans; these will be covered when the separate pieces are appliquéd in place.

8. The wallhanging is now ready for the decorative details. Add lace and ribbon, tacking them down securely. Cover the seams with Victorian stitches (see Stitch Dictionary, page 63). Add floral designs and spiderwebs on solid-colored fabrics.

9. Clip and turn under the seam allowances of the medallion; then press them flat. Position the medallion carefully over the basework and pin it in place. With a blind stitch, appliqué the medallion onto the base. Do the same for each of the corner fans. Press the whole piece, making sure everything lies nice and flat. Carefully measure and trim the base piece down to 21" x 31".

WALLHANGING
FAN
PATTERN

10. Now add beading, buttons, and doodads.

11. Add borders in desired manner, using a ¼" seam allowance. Trim excess fabric at corners.

12. Cut the backing fabric to 28½" x 38½" and pin it to the quilt. Tack backing to front by taking small hidden stitches from the front. (You can hide these under the lace and embroidery stitches.)

13. Cut the binding fabric into four 3"-wide strips, keeping the same length as the borders. Fold each strip in half lengthwise with right sides out, so it is 1½" wide. With the raw edges neatly together, press the fold along the length of the strip.

14. Match the raw edges of the binding with the raw edge of the border, right sides together. Machine stitch a ½"-wide seam through all layers. Turn the binding over the raw seams to the back. Whipstitch the binding to the backing by hand. Corners can be square or mitered.

15. A good method to display a wallhanging is on a rod or dowel that fits into a tube or sleeve sewn to the back of the quilt. You need a fabric rectangle 6½" x 30" for a sleeve. On each short end, turn under ½" allowance and machine stitch along the raw edge. Now fold the strip in half lengthwise, matching long edges. The strip is now 3¼" wide. Sew the long edges with a ¼" seam, then turn the piece right side out and press with the seam in the center. Pin the sleeve to the backing, just below the binding edge at the top of the quilt, centered ½" from each side. Whipstitch the sleeve to the backing at the edges of the sleeve.

From tea cozies to Christmas stockings, pendants, and purses—Judith enjoys crazy quilting them all.

Doll blanket made by the author. Courtesy Gloria McKinnon

Pouch made by the author using ribbons courtesy of Mokuba Ribbons. Beadwork was added as a gift to the author by Susan Clark.

Madeleine Montano, from small girl to lovely young woman. Photos by Bill O'Connor

Stitch Dictionary

This is a dictionary of stitches and motifs commonly used in crazy quilting. Once you have mastered the basics, you can go on to the variations. Most often embroidery stitches are used to cover seam lines on base work, but they can also be used as decorative elements anywhere on the piece. Combined with ribbon, beads, and other embellishments, they make crazy quilting lively. "Adding Other Stitches" shows how to combine stitches. Combinations of stitches work well in crazy quilting because they add so much color and design. By using different colored thread for each step, you can create wonderful highlights in your work. Try the combinations illustrated, then try your own. Remember that repetition of stitches is an important element in good design.

Straight Stitch

Come up at A and go down at B, making the stitch the desired length; pull the thread firmly in place. Straight stitches can be worked evenly or irregularly. They can vary in length and direction, but do not make the stitches too loose or too long or they could snag.

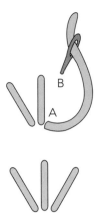

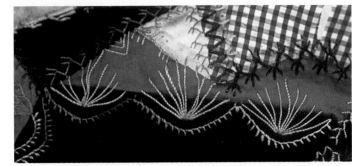

Couching

Couching is a decorative way to hold a long (laid) thread in place. Mark a line the desired length of the couching stitch. Position the laid thread along the designated line. Now with either matching or contrasting thread or ribbon, come up at A and go down at B wrapping a small, tight stitch over the laid thread at regular intervals.

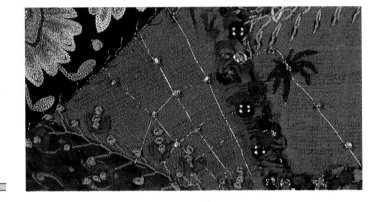

Colonial Knot

This lovely little knot sits up and has a little dimple in the center. Come up at A. Work the thread to form a loop starting *over* the needle head and ending *under* the needle tip; this forms a figure "8." Hold the needle upright and pull the thread firmly around the needle. Insert the needle at B (as close to A as possible, but not into it). Hold the knot in place until the needle is worked completely through the fabric. Example: rose buds, muscari (tiny flower clusters).

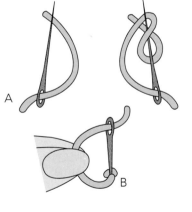

French Knot

Come up at A and wrap the thread twice around the needle. While holding the thread taut, go down at B (as close to A as possible, but not into it). Hold the knot in place until the needle is completely through the fabric.

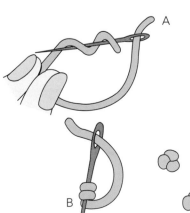

Buttonhole Stitch

Work this stitch from left to right. Come up at A, hold the thread down with your thumb, and go down at B, emerging at C. Bring the needle tip over the thread and pull into place. The bottom line formed should lie on the seam line; keep the vertical stitches straight and even.

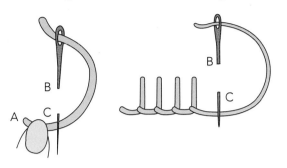

Variations

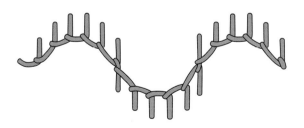

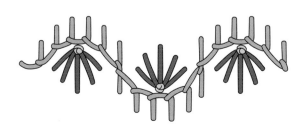

Adding Other Stitches

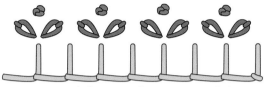

Buttonhole + French Knot + Lazy Daisy

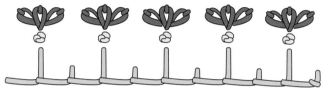

Buttonhole + French Knot + Lazy Daisy

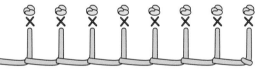

Buttonhole + French Knot + Cross Stitch

Closed Buttonhole

This stitch is similar to the regular buttonhole, except that two vertical stitches are worked into the same hole. This forms the triangle shapes

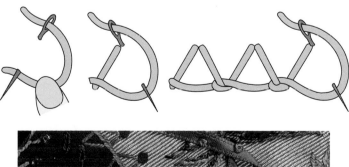

Satin Stitch

Satin stitch was a favorite of Victorian crazy quilters. It can be worked in single or double layers to create a thick, smooth blanket of stitching. The stitch can be worked straight up and down, side to side, or at an angle, laying down straight stitches close together to conform to the outlined shape.

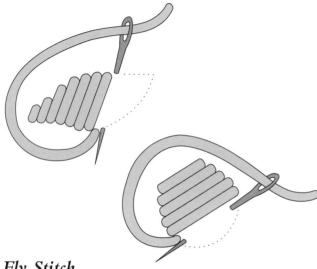

Fly Stitch

Come up at A, go down at B (even with and to the right of A), and emerge at C bringing the needle tip over the thread. Draw the thread gently through the fabric. Go down at D (the desired length of the stitch) forming a catch stitch.

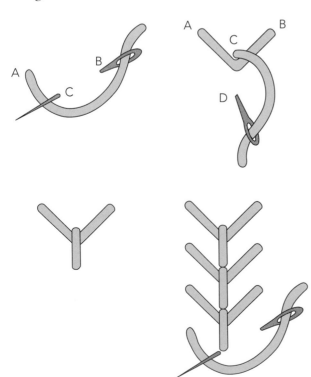

Herringbone Stitch

The Herringbone stitch is worked from left to right and lies evenly on both sides of the seam. It is created by taking a small horizontal backstitch on each side of the seam. Be sure to keep the horizontal stitches even, as this creates the design.

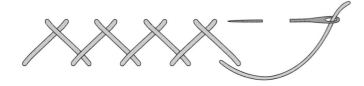

Variations

Adding Other Stitches

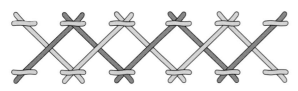

Herringbone + Running Stitch

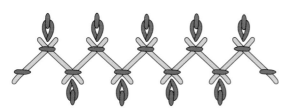

Herringbone + Running Stitch + Lazy Daisy

Herringbone + French Knots

Herringbone + Single Stitch + Lazy Daisy

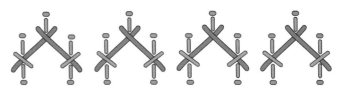

Elongated Herringbone + Beads + Running Stitch

Feather Stitch

This stitch begins with a single Feather stitch and alternates back and forth. The feather stitch is a vertical stitch and is worked down toward you. The only secret to this stitch is to remember to always put the needle in at B, straight across from where the thread came out at A.

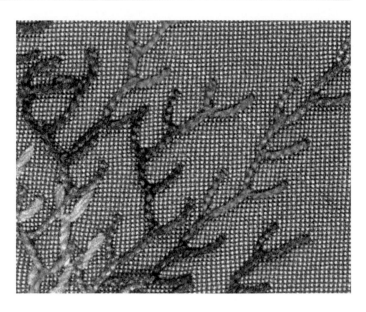

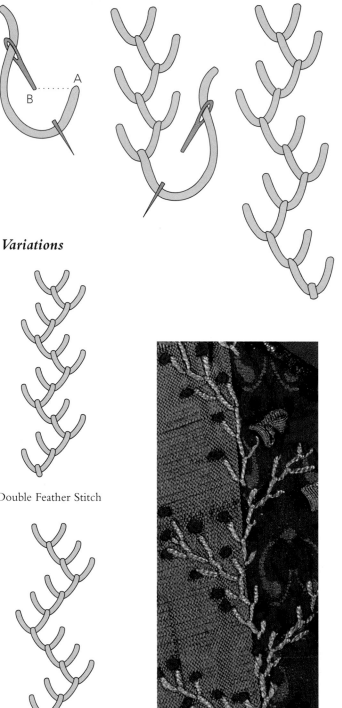

Variations

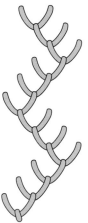

Double Feather Stitch

Triple Feather Stitch

Adding Other Stitches

Feather Stitch
+
Lazy Daisy
+
Straight Stitch

Feather Stitch
+
Beads

Feather Stitch
+
Lazy Daisy
+
French Knot

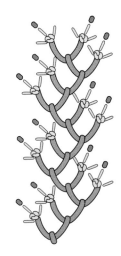

Feather Stitch (double)
+
Straight Stitch
+
Beads
+
French Knot

Chevron Stitch

This is another stitch that lies horizontally and evenly on each side of a seam. It is worked left to right. Start in the lower corner and take a short stitch forward, then a half stitch back. Work the same stitch on the upper line just a little to the right. Work this stitch alternately from one side to the other. Be sure to keep the small backstitches evenly spaced.

Adding Other Stitches

Chevron + French Knot + Lazy Daisy

Chevron + Lazy Daisy + Straight Stitch

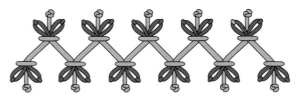

Chevron + Lazy Daisy + Straight Stitch
+ Bead or French Knot

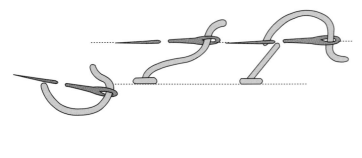

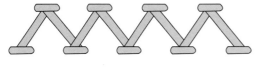

Variations

Cretan Stitch

The Cretan stitch starts in the bottom left corner and is worked from left to right. Short vertical stitches are worked alternately downward and upward. Hold the thread down so the needle will pass over it. This stitch should be worked evenly on each side of a seam. Be sure to keep the vertical stitches even.

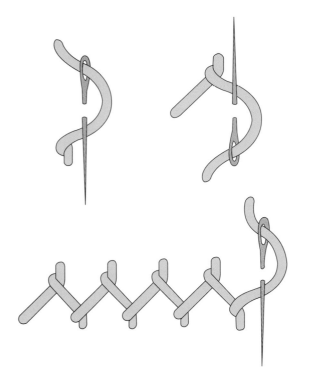

Variations

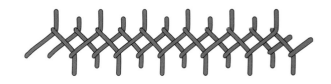

Adding Other Stitches

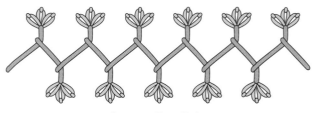

Cretan + French Knot + Straight Stitch

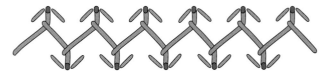

Cretan + Lazy Daisy

Cretan + Straight Stitch + Bead

Lazy Daisy Stitch

The Lazy Daisy is a looped stitch, like a free-floating chain stitch. It can be worked in rows or used randomly. Bring the thread up through the fabric. Hold it down with your thumb and insert the needle again at the starting point. Bring it out a short distance away, making sure the needle comes over the thread. Now take a small holding stitch at the top of the loop.

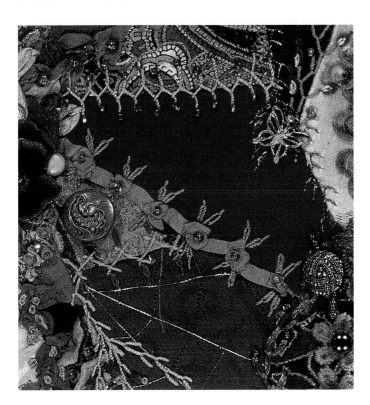

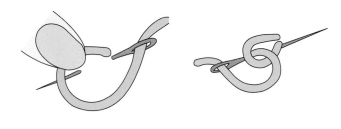

Variations

Adding Other Stitches

Lazy Daisy + French Knots

Lazy Daisy (one short and one long) + Straight Stitch + Beads

Lazy Daisy + Straight Stitch + French Knot or Bead

Lazy Daisy + French Knot + Straight Stitch

Chain Stitch

The Chain stitch is similar to the Lazy Daisy except that it is continuous. Pull up the thread at the starting point and hold it down with your finger. Bring the needle down into the starting point and come up again a short distance away. Be sure the needle comes up over the thread, forming a loop. Repeat to make a chain.

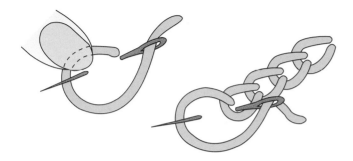

Running Stitch

The Running stitch is worked from right to left. Make small, even stitches. The stitch that shows should be the same width as the spaces.

Stem Stitch

The Stem stitch works from left to right. Sew along the stitch line and keep the thread to the left of the needle. Take small, even stitches. When laying stitch lines side by side to fill in an area, be sure to fit them snugly in order to cover.

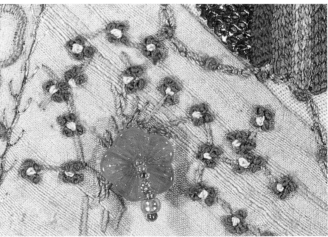

Fans

Embroidered fans are a traditional decorative touch in crazy quilting. They are very effective used in a row to cover seam lines or enlarged to act as a highlight. Be sure to pull the threads firmly into place. Otherwise they will snag and lose their shapes.

Combining Stitches

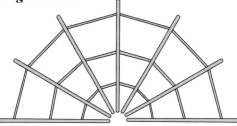

Straight Stitches + Running Stitches

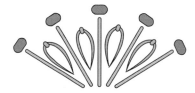

Straight Stitches + Cross Stitches

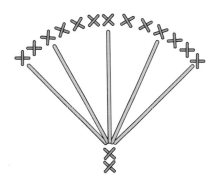

Straight Stitches + Beads + Lazy Daisy

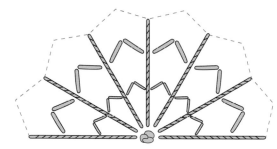

Stem Stitches + Running Stitch + French Knot

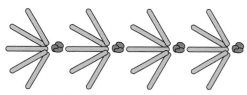

Straight Lines + French Knots

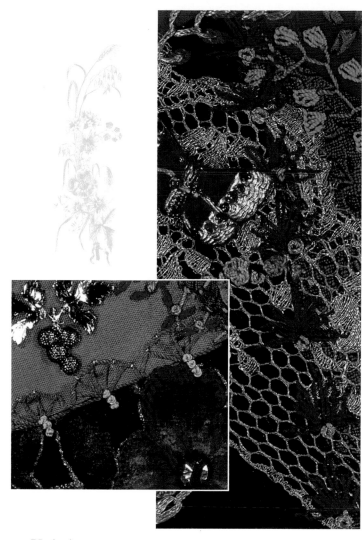

Variations

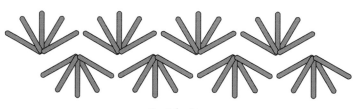

Straight Lines

Lazy Daisies

Straight Lines

73

Webs

What is a crazy quilt without a spider and its web? This is a favorite embroidery motif. Metallic and iridescent threads make them terrific. A good quality of metallic thread will not unravel. Using short threads will help prevent the unraveling problem, too. Some metallics are wrapped around a thread core and will break away if used too roughly. All spokes of the webs shown are couched down. Try using a smooth spun metallic thread for the couching stitches.

Corner Web

Four Intersecting Spokes

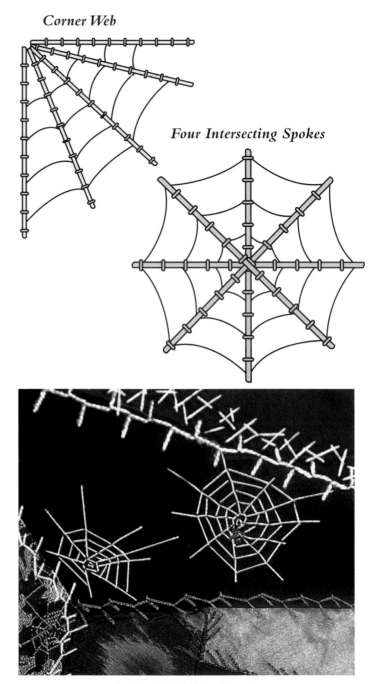

Six-Spoke Web with Continuous Thread

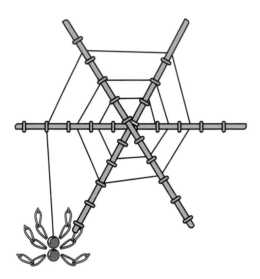

Spiders

Spiders are a unique, very traditional part of crazy quilting. In Europe, they are considered good luck when worked into needlework. But it can be difficult to make them look nice. Many compromise to make them with six legs instead of eight. Each leg is made of two chain stitches connected to a body made of two iridescent beads.

Free-Form Trees

This is a good example of experimenting with
and combining stitches. The tree I use most is made
of Feather stitch, Stem and Chain stitches. The trunk
and branches are Stem and Chain, laid closely
together to act as fillers and to give the
illusion of a bark-like texture. A variety of colors creates shading. The Feather stitches are random,
to represent leaves and twigs. Make the Feather
stitches uneven and free. Adding beads creates
further highlights.

Combining other stitches can create different
kinds of trees. The examples below show combinations of Lazy Daisy, Satin and Straight stitches that
create trees with widely different "personalities."
Willow, bonsai, apple and other types of trees can
be wonderful highlights in crazy quilting.

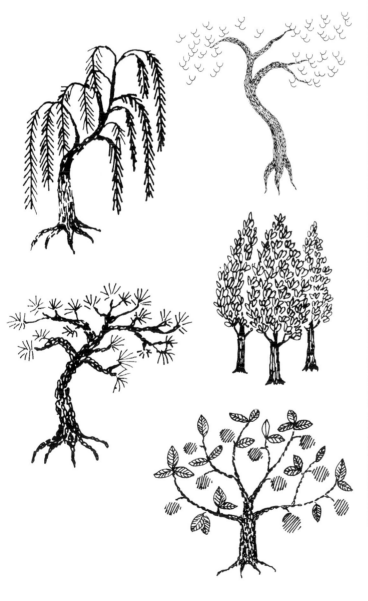

Study in Dusties by the author. Photo by Judith Baker Montano

Study in Jewel Tones by the author. Photo by Judith Baker Montano

Left-Handed Stitches

At last, a section just for left handers! Study the diagrams and read the written instructions carefully before starting. If you want to try other stitches not shown in this section, try holding the book upside down. Once the needle is inserted into the fabric, use the middle finger of your right hand at the fabric back to help guide the needle to the fabric front. When the needle tip appears on the fabric surface, you can easily grasp it with your left hand to continue the next stitch. If you take a class, always sit in front of the instructor to observe the stitches.

Buttonhole Stitch

Work this stitch from right to left. Come up at A and hold the thread down with your thumb. Go down at B and emerge at C. Bring the needle tip over the thread and pull into place. The bottom line formed should lie on the seam line; keep the vertical stitches straight and even.

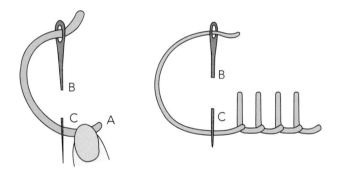

Chain Stitch

Come up at A and form a loop. Go down at B (as close to A as possible, but not into it) and emerge at C bringing the needle tip over the thread. Repeat this stitch to make a chain.

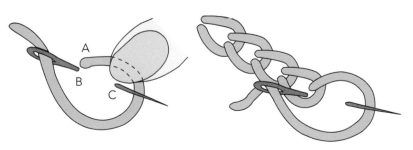

Chevron Stitch

Work the stitch from right to left along two parallel lines. Come up at A, go down at B, and emerge at C (the center of the stitch). Make a straight stitch the desired length to D, insert the needle, and emerge at E. Go down at F (equal to the length of AB) and emerge at G. Continue working, alternating from one side to the other and keeping the stitches evenly spaced.

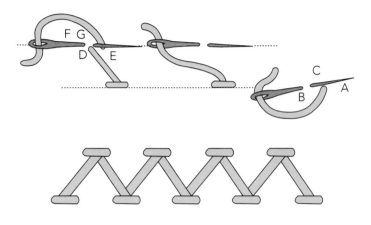

Colonial Knot

Come up at A. Work the thread to form a loop starting over the needle head and ending under the needle tip. This forms a figure "8." Hold the needle upright and pull the thread firmly around the needle. Insert the needle at B (as close to A as possible, but not into it) and hold the knot in place until the needle is worked completely through the fabric.

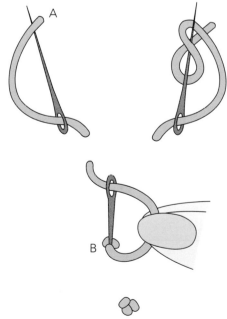

Cretan Stitch

Work this stitch, from right to left, along two parallel lines. Come up at A, go down at B, and emerge at C taking a downward vertical stitch the desired length and bringing the needle tip over the thread. Insert at D and emerge at E, taking an upward vertical stitch. Be sure to keep the vertical stitches evenly spaced.

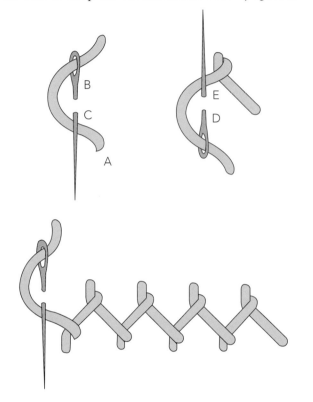

Feather Stitch

Come up at A, go down at B (even with and to the right of A), and emerge at C. Alternate the stitches back and forth, working them downwards in a vertical column.

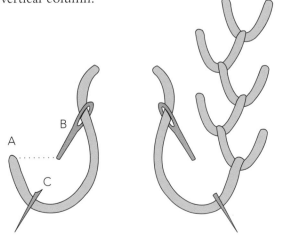

French Knot

Come up at A and wrap the thread twice around the needle. While holding the thread taut, go down at B (as close to A as possible, but not into it). Hold the knot in place until the needle is completely through the fabric.

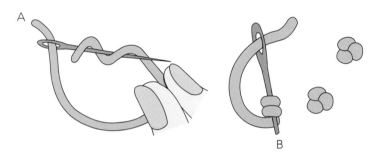

Herringbone Stitch

Work the stitch from right to left. Come up at A, go down at B, and emerge at C, taking a small horizontal backstitch. Continue working, alternating from side to side.

Stem Stitch

Work this stitch from right to left. Mark a line the desired length of the Stem stitch. Sew along the line keeping the thread below the needle. Take small even stitches. When laying stitch lines side by side to fill in an area, be sure fit them snugly in order to cover.

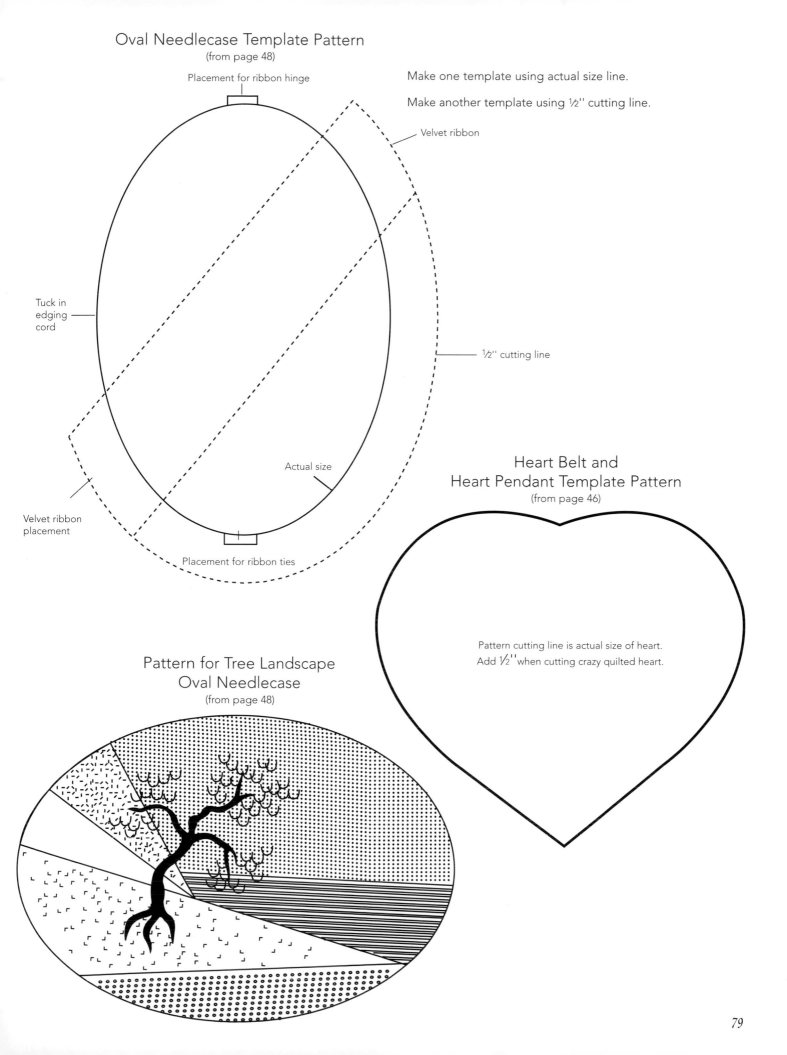

Oval Needlecase Template Pattern
(from page 48)

Placement for ribbon hinge

Make one template using actual size line.

Make another template using ½'' cutting line.

Velvet ribbon

Tuck in edging cord

½'' cutting line

Actual size

Velvet ribbon placement

Placement for ribbon ties

Heart Belt and Heart Pendant Template Pattern
(from page 46)

Pattern cutting line is actual size of heart. Add ½'' when cutting crazy quilted heart.

Pattern for Tree Landscape Oval Needlecase
(from page 48)

Index

Bibliography

Aikman, Susanne Z.
    A Primer: The Art of Native American Beadwork
    1980, Morning Flower Press, Denver, CO

Bond, Dorothy
    Crazy Quilt Stitches
    1981, Self-Published, Cottage Grove, OR

Haywood, Dixie
    Crazy Quilting with a Difference
    1981, Dover Publications, Inc., New York, NY

McMorris, Penny
    Crazy Quilts
    1984, E.P. Dutton, New York, NY

Montano, Judith Baker
    The Crazy Quilt Handbook
    1986, C&T Publishing, Inc., Lafayette, CA
    Crazy Quilt Odyssey (out of print)
    1991, C&T Publishing, Inc., Lafayette, CA
    The Art of Silk Ribbon Embroidery
    1993, C&T Publishing, Inc., Lafayette, CA
    Recollections
    1993, C&T Publishing, Inc., Lafayette, CA
    Elegant Stitches
    1995, C&T Publishing, Inc., Lafayette, CA
    Judith Baker Montano: Art & Inspirations
    1997, C&T Publishing, Inc., Lafayette, CA
    Floral Stitches
    2000, C&T Publishing, Inc., Lafayette, CA

Videos
    Crazy Quilting
    1996, C&T Publishing, Inc., Lafayette, CA
    Silk Ribbon Embroidery
    1996, C&T Publishing, Inc., Lafayette, CA
    Embellishments
    1997, C&T Publishing, Inc., Lafayette, CA
    Landscapes
    1998, C&T Publishing, Inc., Lafayette, CA

Nichols, Marion
    Encyclopedia of Embroidery Stitches, Including Crewel
    1974, Dover Publications, New York, NY

For more information write for a free catalog:

C&T Publishing, Inc.
P. O. Box 1456
Lafayette, CA 94549
(800) 284-1114
e-mail: ctinfo@ctpub.com
website: www.ctpub.com

For quilting supplies:

Cotton Patch Mail Order
3405 Hall Lane, Dept. CTB
Lafayette, CA 94549
(800) 835-4418
(925) 283-7883
e-mail: quiltusa@yahoo.com
website: www.quiltusa.com